All About
Memory Albums

The Album Page Designers

We are grateful to the following people for creating the 209 album pages which appear in this book. Some of these designers work for manufacturers who supply products for memory albums, some have scrapbooking retail stores (see page 144) and some are simply individuals who love scrapbooking. We're proud to feature their cute, pretty, charming and gorgeous album pages. In alphabetical order, they are:

- ❖ **Amberly Beck**, Lewiston, Idaho
- ❖ **Amber Blakesley** for Paper Hearts
- ❖ **Dawn Chapman** for Memory Lane
- ❖ **Amy Clegern**, Bellevue, Washington
- ❖ **Nancy Church** for Pebbles in My Pocket
- ❖ **Erika Clayton** for Pebbles in My Pocket
- ❖ **Lynn Damelio** for Rubber Stampede®
- ❖ **Carrie DuWelius** for Memory Lane
- ❖ **Sandi Genovese** for Ellison® Craft & Design
- ❖ **LeNae Gerig** for Hot Off The Press
- ❖ **Becky Goughnour** for Hot Off The Press
- ❖ **Katie Hacker** for Hot Off The Press
- ❖ **Debbie Hewitt**, Agoura, California
- ❖ **Heather Hummel**, Salt Lake City, Utah
- ❖ **Sherri Johnston** for Pebbles in My Pocket
- ❖ **Marci Kearns**, Woodburn, Oregon
- ❖ **Kim McCrary** for Pebbles in My Pocket
- ❖ **Karen McGavin** for Pebbles in My Pocket
- ❖ **Allison Myers** for Memory Lane
- ❖ **Launa Naylor** for Pebbles in My Pocket
- ❖ **Debbie Peterson**, Kennewick, Washington

- ❖ **Bridgette Server** for Memories & More™
- ❖ **Kim Skinner** for Memory Lane
- ❖ **Ann Smith** for Memory Lane
- ❖ **Carla Spence** for C.M. Offray & Son, Inc.
- ❖ **Anne-Marie Spencer** for Hot Off The Press
- ❖ **Grace Taormina** for Rubber Stampede®
- ❖ **Stephanie Taylor**, Valencia, California

Hot Off The Press Production Credits:

Project editors:	Tara Choate
	Mary Margaret Hite
Technical editors:	LeNae Gerig
	Becky Goughnour
Photographer:	Kevin Laubacher
Graphic designers:	Sally Clarke
	Jacie Pete
	Susan Shea
Digital imagers:	Victoria Gleason
	Larry Seith
Editors:	Paulette Jarvey
	Kris Andrews
	Lynda Hill
	Tom Muir

published by

P.O. Box 55595
Little Rock, Arkansas 72215

produced by

Library of Congress catalog numer 98-66057
Hardcover ISBN 1-57486-095-X
Softcover ISBN 1-57486-093-3

Canby, Oregon USA

All About
Memory Albums

little girls are heaven's flowers

Jenny~
JUNE 8, 1996
Her wedding day....

Table of Contents

Each of us has memories to save and stories to tell. Making memory albums gives us the opportunity to do both. It's all about getting those precious photos into albums where they can be seen and shared. This book is full of excellent ideas for honoring every photo in those shoe boxes! The ideas in each chapter can be used within every other chapter. There are some great ideas in Special Days that would work well with childhood photos and there are some beautiful techniques in Black & White that would create great effects for ancestral baby photos. The pages in this book provide specific details on each technique.

We do have one caution: Making memory albums is addictive! You may want to make an album for each child or make a smaller album dedicated to a special vacation or one exclusively for Christmases. Also, an album is a uniquely wonderful gift. We invite you to join us in an extremely satisfying activity that will be treasured for years to come by yourself and by those you love. Best of all, you possess all that is necessary—photos and a caring for the memories of your life.

Introduction

Baby

Childhood

School, Sports & Teens

Wedding

Unveil those wedding photos with flair! Whether your wedding is wild and wacky, quiet and traditional or flowery and romantic these pages will give you ideas on how to show them to their best advantage. This chapter will show you how to use your wedding colors on every page to create a coordinated album that will enhance every detail of that memorable day

Christmas

No season produces more photos than Christmas; however, with practically the same background in each, sometimes it's hard to tell one year's photos from another! There are enough ideas featured in this chapter to make each year's pictures unique! Rubber stamping, adhesive ribbon and scene-making techniques are also outlined

Special Days

From New Year's Day to Hanukkah, if it's a day that's important to you these ideas can help you make the page special. Birthdays also received distinctive treatement, providing ideas from childhood well into adulthood. Special photos get center stage using offset matting, die cuts and interactive techniques (see pages 102 & 105)! The inspirations don't end here!

Vacation

Anything goes in this chapter! We show you some terrific techniques that will make touring your vacation photos a trip! Learn how to "split" a page, make a "log" mat and use stationery on your page. Vacations are a break from the normal and this section focuses on techniques that are just a little out of the norm!

Portraits & Pets

Sure, a portrait will capture your image, but it does nothing to express your uniqueness! This chapter will illustrate techniques to animate that posed look. We also feature ideas to convey your pet's disposition using templates, journaling and simple patterns.

Black & White

In honor of our ancestors we wrap up this book with techniques to glorify our grandparents with the respect they deserve. We also show great ways to echo the era of the photo with design enhancement. From the 1890's to the 1990's, the ideas in this chapter will show you how to span the grey area between your Black & White photos and the color of our products!

Introduction

Our mission is to make it easier for you to reproduce the techniques you will see in this book. The next few pages show you the products that are available and explain some of the basic techniques such as cropping and matting that are so important in the art of scrapbooking. "What must I have?" "What will be nice to have?" "How did they do that?" All of these questions will be answered in this chapter.

Throughout this book you will hear about memory album tools and products. This chapter will help to define them. For instance, the tools you will see on pages 8–11 were created to enhance your photos regardless of the age or activity of the people in the photos. Punches, die cuts and papers come in all designs to embellish all sorts of themes, moods and events. Patterned scissors can give a silly cut like a dragon's back or produce a sophisticated Victorian edge. These products will allow you to get as goofy or as solemn as you want!

Pages 12–17 describe how to construct a page, crop a photo and make a photo mat. We will relieve you of any worries about accidentally cutting off your father's head or messing up four papers trying to make a perfect square. Then on pages 24 and 25, we show you the difference that background papers make—and they make an impressive difference, indeed.

In pages 18–23, we talk about journaling. While we often say that our photos have a story to tell, we know that photographs don't actually talk. That's why we stress the importance of journaling. It can be done on a die cut, or directly on the page. Journaling can take the place of embellishments, or be used to enhance them. You'll find six easy-to-learn writing styles and each was designed to help you feel more confident about journaling in your own handwriting. So get your photos and your scissors and read on! More is definitely to come.

Tools

What must I have? In making memory albums you'll use paper, scissors and glue. Acid-free is the watchword in this activity. Items so labeled have a neutral pH and will not cause your photos to deteriorate any faster than nature allows. Use only acid- and lignin-free papers, glues, stickers, die cuts, pens, and sheet protectors. There are pH pens which can be used to tell you the acidic content of unlabeled products. With this activity becoming so popular, manufacturers are racing to determine the acidity of their products and label them as such.

Acid-free adhesive:

This includes stick glue, liquid glue, double-stick adhesive sheets or squares, corner mounts, or tape runners (with pieces of double-stick tape on a roll)—just be sure the label says acid-free.

Acid-free black pens:

Many widths are available; a medium tip, .03 or .05, is a good all-purpose size. Or choose a pen with two tips, allowing you to use a thick or a thin line.

Templates:

To begin it's best to have a few basic templates with several sizes of circles, ovals, hearts and stars. Some templates have a decorative ruler on the edge.

Album or Binder:

There are lots of choices and at least two sizes, 8½"x11" and 12"x12. Three-ring binders allow you to easily add or rearrange pages. Do NOT use "magnetic" albums, which may not have acid-free sheets and can destroy photos. Be sure all interior sheets are acid-free and lignin-free.

Scissors:
Straight scissors

Pattern-edged scissors:
It's great to have one or more pattern-edged styles. You can add other designs as you create album pages. Corner edgers are a new type of scissors designed to create distinctive corners on photos or mats.

Plain Papers:
Plain papers are available by the sheet, in packages by color assortment or in book form. They need to be acid-free and lignin-free.

Patterned Papers:
Patterned papers, like plain papers, are sold individually, in packages, or in books by theme. They too must be acid-free and lignin-free. The most common sizes are 8½"x11" and 12"x12" papers. Many manufacturer's feature color-coordination in their paper packages, making it even easier to create spectacular pages.

Sheet Protectors:
Sheet protectors fit 8½"x11" or 12"x12" pages. They can be top-loading or side-loading. Be sure they are acid-free—never use any made of vinyl.

And More Tools

What would be nice to have? As you create album pages, you may want to add to your tool box with a wider selection of the must-have items listed on page 8–9—more pattern-edged scissors, templates and papers. As you go through the chapters of this book you'll find lots of "nice-to-haves." They include the items on these pages as well as items such as red-eye pens (to remove the red glare in flash photos), pet-eye pens (to remove the glare from animals' eyes), pH pens (to test acidity), colored pens, doilies and more. New products are appearing on the market everyday!

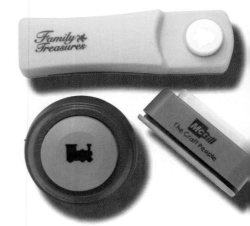

Punches:

Punches come in a variety of shapes and styles. Some only cut corners or page edges while others are "long-handled" to allow you to punch further into the page.

Die Cuts:

Die cuts are available in themed packages or you can make your own using a die cutting machine. Many stores allow you to use their machine if you buy the paper there or for a nominal fee.

Stickers:

Stickers are a memory album staple. They now come in so many themes and motifs that you can find some to complement *any* page.

Lettering Template:

Lettering templates are becoming widely available in many styles. They are effective for creating spectacular headlines for your pages.

Rubber Stamps:

Rubber stamps are a familiar craft tool that have only recently been introduced to scrapbooking. There is an endless variety of stamps available.

All Night Media®, Inc.

All Night Media®, Inc.

Rubber Stampede®

Marvy® Uchida

Rubber Stampede®

Punch-Outs™:

Punch-Outs™ are a wonderful graphic embellishment for any page. There is a wide variety of theme books. The graphics easily punch out of these books.

Photo Corners:

Photo Corners have been used for years to make scrapbooks. They can be used only for decoration or to attach your photo if you don't care to use glue.

Rulers:

Rulers are very valuable and they should be one of the first things to add to your tool box. Use the plain edge for making straight mats, the ruler for measuring and the patterned edge for splitting pages or drawing patterns.

Corrugator:

Corrugators add depth and texture to your pages. Insert the paper or die cut into the machine, turn the handle and let the object come out the other side.

Stencils:

Stencils are different than templates, though they look alike and sometimes can be used in a similar manner. Stencils are usually more intricate and are designed for painting or drawing. They can be used in memory albums like templates.

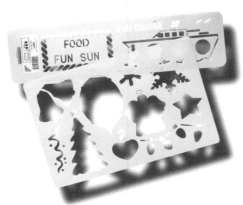

Page Construction

How did they do that? Here are the basic steps to creating an album page. You'll need the tools listed on pages 8–9 and may want to add a few listed on pages 10–11.

Where to start? It's best to begin with your most recent photos. Chances are you'll know where they were taken and remember the names of everyone in each photo! Then work back in time to organize photos of the past by date or event.

Throughout this book you'll find references to the "focal point" of a page. The focal point is simply that item on the page which attracts your eye. A page without a clear focal point lacks impact.

1 Select your photos based on the theme, event or some common thread.

2 Choose plain and patterned papers to complement your photos and embellish your theme.

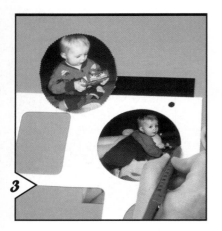

3 Crop your photos (more about this on page 14–15). This is where you'll use patterned scissors and templates. Here a plastic template helps make a perfect circle, while another photo has already been cropped with patterned scissors.

4 Mat your photos with plain or patterned paper (pages 16–17 go into more detail about matting). Glue the cropped photos to the paper and cut ⅛"–½" away using plain or pattern-edged scissors.

5 Arrange the photos on the page. The eye naturally "reads" a page following a figure Z. By creating a focal point and placing photos along the Z, you control the order in which the page is viewed. Mix sizes and shapes for an interesting arrangement.

6 Add decorative elements— punches, stickers, die cuts, etc. These balloons are die cuts by Ellison® Craft & Design. Note the Z figure is followed by the die cuts. Also notice the elements overlap, adding interest to the page.

7 Write a description of the person, action or events shown in the photos. This is called "journaling" and is very important in order to make your album a book of memories, rather than just a collection of photographs. Write directly on the album page or onto a piece of paper which is then glued to the page. You can journal in your own handwriting, with a computer or typewriter, press-on letters, stickers or other aids. Read more about journaling on pages 18–23.

8 Slip the finished album page into an acid-free sheet protector, then into your album or binder. Many sheet protectors fit 8½"x11" papers, but 12"x12" sheet protectors are coming into the market.

Making album pages should be a fun way to capture memories for the future; don't turn it into a chore! Most of the pages in your album should take only 5–10 minutes to complete. You may want to spend more time on some special photos or memories of a special time, but many photos almost speak for themselves. (Just don't leave out the important details of when and where.)

Keep the activity fun. Don't spend two hours creating the perfect album page unless you have that kind of time. Perhaps you'll embellish only half your album pages. Helpful hint: Use a sheet of patterned paper (the kind with all over designs) as the background and you won't need to do much embellishing. Keep it manageable so you'll continue saving those memories!

Cropping

By cutting (also called "cropping") photos to show only the most important parts, you'll be able to get more photos on a page and they'll be more interesting. If you're unsure about cropping, make color copies and practice on those. It's really easy! **Tip:** When cutting, it's easier to turn the photo rather than the scissors.

1 Leave historical items like houses, cars or furniture—they'll be fun to see years from now.

2 Trim close to the focal person or thing. Use straight or pattern-edged scissors.

3 Use a plastic template for smooth ovals, perfect circles and great shapes. Place the template on top of the photo and mark with a pen or a grease pencil. Cut inside the line. Lots of shapes are available.

4 For another look, cut a **silhouette** by cutting along the edge of the focal point, removing all the background. Don't worry, you don't have to cut perfectly. It's a great look that allows the focal point of the photo to become important on your album page.

5 It's fun to **bump out** one section of the photo by silhouetting one area, but leaving the rest of the photo with a background. Look at this bunny's ears and the baby's feet. Some other "bump-able" examples are balloons, elbows, hats—there are many examples in the photos in this book.

6 **Cropping Polaroid photos:** Older photos (8–10 years old) may separate when cut from their white bindings, but this isn't harmful to them (or to you). If you include part of the white seam just above the writing plaque, the photo is less likely to separate. Newer photos taken on Spectra film do not separate so easily; however, years of bending on flexible album pages might cause separation. You can use the same cropping technique for them, or the pieces can be held together with a sheet protector. Before cropping a just-taken Polaroid, wait 10–15 minutes after it develops so it is completely dry. Never cut into the white envelope at the bottom of the photo—this is where the developer is located.

7 If you're hesitant about cropping older or one-of-a-kind photos, make a color copy (a color copy is best even for black & white photos; just be sure to copy onto acid-free and lignin-free paper). Then cut the copy for your album.

uncropped original

cropped color photocopy

8 Mat your photos using the techniques on pages 16–17.

You don't have to crop every photo. Use your best judgement—does the photo need a clear focal point? Is there a lot of "extra" background? Does your page need the variety of differently shaped photos? Cropping is only one tool in your repertoire.

Matting

Matting is the heart and soul of scrapbooking. Matting can be used on nearly any page element—photos, die cuts, Punch-Outs™ . . . even backgrounds can be matted. Throughout this book, we give directions to mat an element using a specific mat width, scissor or color. Steps 1–8 include basic directions as well as explanations of the most used matting techniques.

1 Glue the cropped photo to a sheet of paper and cut ¹⁄₈"–¹⁄₂" away, forming a mat. Use plain or patterned paper for the mat. Use straight-edged scissors...

2 ...or pattern-edged scissors for one or both cuts. It's fun to mix and match cuts.

3 Double- or triple-mat some photos. Try adding even more mats for special photos, such as portraits. Vary mat sizes, using narrow (¹⁄₈") and wide (¹⁄₂"–1") mats, as well as standard (¹⁄₄") sizes.

4 Mix straight-edged and pattern-edged scissors on your photos and mats. Photos cropped using patterned scissors and matted with plain scissors provide the impression of an "extra" matting layer.

5 Mix your mat shapes, perhaps matting an oval inside a rectangle.

6 Keep the mats for bumped-out photos simple and cut close to the edge.

7 For a different look, offset mat a photo. Cut the mat in the same shape and size of the photo, then glue it to one side instead of centered under the photo. Notice that the mat resembles a shadow. Another look is to tilt the mat behind the photo.

8 For a great look, journal on a wide mat! Add other embellishments—stickers, punches, etc.—as inspiration strikes.

Of course, these are not the only techniques and looks you'll see! Always plan ahead before making your cuts. Often it's helpful to use a ruler to draw guides before actually cutting so your lines are straight. This is especially important when using straight scissors—there is nothing like a crooked line to ruin a mat!

Ball & Stick with Punch!

Stick lettering is the basic form for most lettering styles. Accented with dots or slashes, it becomes spectacular. Yet, it is the most simple style to do. This page shows stick lettering embellished with punched circles and outlined with a •—•— border. (Tub pattern on page 140.)

¼" **and** ½" **Round Punches:** Marvy® Uchida
Bathtub and Bubbles Die Cut: Accu/Cut® Systems
Big Bubbles Patterned Paper: *Paper Pizazz™ Childhood Memories* by Hot Off The Press
Scissors: Scallop Paper Edgers by Fiskars®, Inc.
Lettering Designer: Becky Goughnour for Hot Off The Press
Page Designer: Katie Hacker for Hot Off The Press

© & ™ Accu/Cut® Systems

A B C D E F G H I J K L M
N O P Q R S T U V W X Y Z
a b c d e f g h i j k l m n o p q r
s t u v w x y z 1 2 3 4 5 6 7 8 9 0

A B C D E F G H I J K L M N
O P Q R S T U V W X Y Z
a b c d e f g h i j k l m n o p q r s t
u v w x y z 1 2 3 4 5 6 7 8 9 0

ABCDEFGHIJK
LMNOPQRSTUV
WXYZ
abcdefghijklm
nopqrstuvwxyz
12345
67890

Block Letters + Embellishments

Block lettering is traced onto colored paper. Before it is cut out, stickers are added to the outline. The letters and stickers are cut out as one and matted with black. Run the letters down one side of the page. Simple stick lettering is used in the journaling block to offset the larger headline.

Patterned Paper: Frances Meyer Inc.®
Scissors: Cloud Paper Edgers by Fiskars®, Inc.
Stickers: Frances Meyer Inc.®
Lettering and Page Designer: Becky Goughnour for Hot Off The Press

ABCDEFGHIJK
LMNOPQRSTU
VWXYZ abcde
fghijklmnopqrstu
vwxyz1234567890

Barnwood Stick Lettering

Instead of curving the letters, a ruler and some imagination are used to create barnwood letters. This style is perfect for rustic pages of all kinds. Notice the journaling square has a —• border which matches the page border.

Barnwood Patterned
Paper: *Paper Pizazz™ Country* by Hot Off The Press
Scissors: Deckle Paper Edgers by Fiskars®, Inc.
Stickers: ©Mrs. Grossman's Paper Co.
Lettering Designer: Becky Goughnour for Hot Off The Press
Page Designer: Katie Hacker for Hot Off The Press

Cattywampus Lettering

The fun of a camping trip is perfectly depicted with irregular and slightly skewed lettering. It's easy to do and nearly mistake proof! After all, who is to say you didn't mean to do that? (Tent pattern on page 139.)

Camping Equipment Patterned Paper: *Paper Pizazz™ Great Outdoors* by Hot Off The Press

Lantern and Tent Die Cuts: Accu/Cut® Systems

Brown and White Pens: Marvy® Uchida

Scissors: Peaks Paper Edgers by Fiskars®, Inc.

Lettering Designer: Becky Goughnour for Hot Off The Press

Page Designer: Katie Hacker for Hot Off The Press

© & ™ Accu/Cut® Systems

A a B b C c D d E e F f G g
H h I i J j K k L l M m N n O o
P p Q q R r S s T t U u V v
W w X x Y y Z z 1 2 3 4 5 6 7
8 9 0

Puff & Stitch Lettering

This lettering style could be used for a baby, quilting, spring or gardening page! Trace the letters onto a page, outline with a pen and cut out. Crop closely and mat each or cut out the entire word as one piece. Also try writing directly on the page. Note how the Punch-Outs™ embellish the theme, leaving no doubt that the lettering is symbolizing infancy rather than any other theme.

Blue & Yellow Plaid Patterned Paper: *Paper Pizazz™ Light Great Backgrounds* by Hot Off The Press

Heart and Pacifier Punch-Outs™: *Paper Pizazz™ Baby Punch-Outs™* by Hot Off The Press

Scissors: Ripple Paper Edgers by Fiskars®, Inc.

Lettering Designer: Becky Goughnour for Hot Off The Press

Page Designer: Katie Hacker for Hot Off The Press

A B C D E F G H I
J K L M N O P Q
R S T U V W X Y Z
1 2 3 4 5 6 7 8 9 0

Swirl & Scroll Lettering

This intricate swirl lettering is really quite simple. Begin with basic lettering, then embellish with swirls until you are satisfied. As always, begin with a pencil and use both large and small letters to accent certain elements. The swirls are a great touch along the page edge, connecting the page elements.

Burgundy, Flower and Teal Handmade Patterned Papers: *Paper Pizazz™ Handmade Papers* by Hot Off The Press

Pansy & Ivy Cutouts: *Paper Pizazz™ Embellishments* by Hot Off The Press

Corner Cutter: Corner Rounder by Marvy® Uchida

Scissors: Ripple Paper Edgers by Fiskars®, Inc.

Gold Pen: ZIG® Opaque Writer by EK Success Ltd.

Lettering and Page Designer: Becky Goughnour for Hot Off The Press

Before & After Using Patterned Paper

"Won't those bright papers overwhelm my photos?" novice scrapbookers ask. "Not unless you let them!" we answer. The most vivid patterns will be broken up and subdued by the photographs, mats and decorative elements you place on your page. The trick is to choose coordinated papers and to be a little daring! The page ideas in this book can help inspire you!

before

after

Color creates fun pages, and patterned papers are an easy way to add it. The same photo arrangement is improved by adding patterned paper matting. The photos are placed on a different patterned paper and Punch-Outs™ are used to add even more color.

Crayons Patterned Paper: *Paper Pizazz™ School Days* by Hot Off The Press
Red with Dots Patterned Paper: *Paper Pizazz™ Bright Great Backgrounds* by Hot Off The Press
Crayon Punch-Outs™: *Paper Pizazz™ School Punch-Outs™* by Hot Off The Press
Scissors: Ripple Paper Edgers by Fiskars®, Inc
Page Designer: LeNae Gerig for Hot Off The Press

This tentative page is improved by adding a patterned paper background. This small change inspired other fun changes, such as the triple-matting, angled photos and Punch-Outs™.

Black Plaid Patterned Paper: Paper Pizazz™ in bulk by Hot Off The Press
Lollipop Punch-Out™: *Paper Pizazz™ Kids Punch-Outs™* by Hot Off The Press
Sun Punch-Out™: *Paper Pizazz™ Holidays & Seasons Punch-Outs™* by Hot Off The Press
Scissors: Scallop Paper Edgers by Fiskars®, Inc
Page Designer: Becky Goughnour for Hot Off The Press

before

after

after

before

Simply adding a themed patterned paper behind exactly the same page elements makes such a difference! The empty areas on the before page are now filled with symbols of the outdoors! In addition, the variety of colors in the patterned paper picks up more colors from the photos.

Moose & Deer Patterned Paper: *Paper Pizazz™ Great Outdoors* by Hot Off The Press

Tree Die Cuts: Ellison® Craft & Design

Scissors: Deckle Paper Edgers by Fiskars®, Inc.

Page Designer: LeNae Gerig for Hot Off The Press

before

after

Adding snowflake patterned paper behind the photos makes a dramatic difference. The large snowflake die cuts echo the smaller snowflake punches, embellishing the theme and adding even more fun to the page!

Snowflakes Patterned Paper: *Paper Pizazz™ Christmas* by Hot Off The Press

Snowflake Punch: Family Treasures

Snowflake Die Cuts: Ellison® Craft & Design

Scissors: Deckle Paper Edgers by Fiskars®, Inc.

Page Designer: Becky Goughnour for Hot Off The Press

26

Baby

This chapter features ideas on how to create a page that will make your baby a star—from matting techniques to design enhancement. Once you start, you'll find that memory album products will quickly become as important as diapers!

Begin by getting creative with punches. This chapter presents ways to combine them to create new shapes! At the top of page 30, hearts, rectangles and circles are pieced together to form a rattle and safety-pin. The top of page 34 combines two hearts and an oval to make candy pieces. The bottom of page 35 uses circles and rectangles to make stoplights which are perfect for this page's theme. In each instance the new shape perfectly complements the background papers and page theme.

A great visual aid is the dimension and texture offered by foam tape. It makes any element literally pop off the page. It's a cute way to call attention to a baby's birth announcement, as shown at the top of page 33. Of course, you'll remember to photocopy the original onto acid-free paper.

Pages 36–39 provide tips for creating a mini-album for your child. Beginning with baby's first photo and including the others in chronological order, you can create a visual story with your photos that will speak as well as any words ever could. See each page entry for specific tips on techniques.

The border for this section was created using Scallop Paper Edgers by Fiskars®, Inc. and a punch from McGill, Inc.

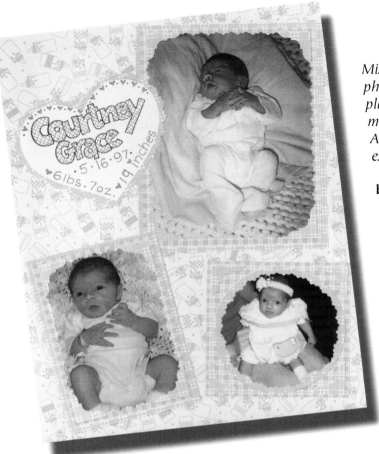

Mix and match scissors when cutting mats. Crop a photo with decorative scissors and cut the mat with plain scissors. Crop a photo in a circle and double-mat it, once in a circle and once in a square shape. Add corners cut with a corner edger to provide an extra layer.

Bottle, Pink Plaid and Blue Plaid Patterned Papers: Paper Patch®
Scissors: Ripple Paper Edgers by Fiskars®, Inc.
Blue Pen: ZIG® Writer by EK Success Ltd.
Pink Pen: ZIG® Opaque Writer by EK Success Ltd.
Corner Cutter: Celestial Corner Edger by Fiskars®, Inc.
Heart Template: Extra Special Products
Page Designer: LeNae Gerig for Hot Off The Press

Contrast is an important part of effective journaling; the trick is to keep your journaling styles consistent in shape. On this page, the words "CHRISTOPHER", "TURNS" and the date are all in the same style. They are separated by "OUR MESSY GUY" in a more ornate style. "ONE" is added in a style similar to the first, but thicker. The effect provides several readings as well as adding a personal touch.

Candle and Cupcake Punch-Outs™: Paper Pizazz™ Celebrations Punch-Outs™ by Hot Off The Press
Candles Patterned Paper: Paper Pizazz™ Birthday Time! by Hot Off The Press
Confetti Patterned Paper: Paper Pizazz™ Birthday by Hot Off The Press
Blue and Red Pens: ZIG® Writer by EK Success Ltd.
Page Designer: Becky Goughnour for Hot Off The Press

Create an L-shaped mat by gluing a trimmed piece of patterned paper onto one side of a plain sheet. Mat three similarly cropped photos, adding a ••—••— border around one mat. Overlap the photos in the top center of the page, then add the blocks below them. Cut out bears from the patterned paper and glue them to connect the elements. Place the matted journaling at the top.

Blocks Patterned Paper: *Paper Pizazz™ Quick & Easy* by Hot Off The Press

It's a Girl and Teddy Bear Patterned Papers: *Paper Pizazz™ Baby* by Hot Off The Press

Scissors: Ripple Paper Edgers by Fiskars®, Inc.

Blue and Red Pens: ZIG® Writer by EK Success Ltd.

Template: Déjà Views™ by C-Thru® Ruler Co.

Page Designer: Debbie Peterson

 Blocks from *Paper Pizazz™ Quick & Easy*

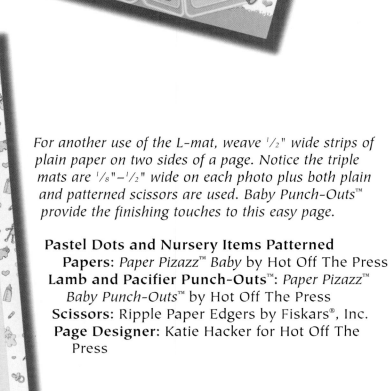

For another use of the L-mat, weave ¹/₂" wide strips of plain paper on two sides of a page. Notice the triple mats are ¹/₈"–¹/₂" wide on each photo plus both plain and patterned scissors are used. Baby Punch-Outs™ provide the finishing touches to this easy page.

Pastel Dots and Nursery Items Patterned Papers: *Paper Pizazz™ Baby* by Hot Off The Press

Lamb and Pacifier Punch-Outs™: *Paper Pizazz™ Baby Punch-Outs™* by Hot Off The Press

Scissors: Ripple Paper Edgers by Fiskars®, Inc.

Page Designer: Katie Hacker for Hot Off The Press

Use creatively grouped punches to decorate your pages. Circle, rectangle and heart punches make a rattle. Cut an oval with decorative scissors and use an oval punch to cut out one end to create a bib. Use circle and rectangle punches to make a safety pin. Large hearts provide an area to journal on.

Pastel Hearts Patterned Paper: *Paper Pizazz™ Baby* by Hot Off The Press

Scissors: Scallop by Family Treasures

Alphabet Stickers: Frances Meyer Inc.®

Bear, Butterfly and Heart Punches: McGill, Inc.

Circle and Rectangle Punches: Family Treasures

Page Designer: Debbie Hewitt

Crop the photos and mat once on green. Place on a piece of white paper (do not glue) and cut another mat. Remove the matted photo. Color a slightly damp make-up sponge with a green marker and drag from the outside edge of the white mat toward the center; let dry. Glue the matted picture to the center. Repeat for the journaling and outer sheet before gluing the matted photos to the candy paper and gluing to the page.

Lollipop Punch-Out™: *Paper Pizazz™ Kids Punch-Outs™* by Hot Off The Press

Rainbow Sweets Patterned Paper: *Paper Pizazz™ Childhood* by Hot Off The Press

Scissors: Deckle Paper Edgers by Fiskars®, Inc.

Green Watercolor Marker: Marvy® Uchida

Stickers: ©Mrs. Grossman's Paper Co.

Page Designer: Debbie Peterson

Stickers are a simple way to express the natural exuberance of youth and draw the eye to your page at the same time. Everyday photos are double-matted on bright plain and patterned papers. Stickers frame the page and journal the theme.

Colorful Stripes Patterned Paper: *Paper Pizazz™ Birthday* by Hot Off The Press

Hearts & Lines Patterned Paper: *Paper Pizazz™ Birthday Time!* by Hot Off The Press

Alphabet and Border Stickers: Frances Meyer Inc.®

Corner Cutter: Corner Rounder by Marvy® Uchida

Page Designer: LeNae Gerig for Hot Off The Press

Trim a piece of pink paper to 5¹⁄₂"x8¹⁄₄" with decorative scissors. Mat with light green and yellow papers. Glue to the center of the pastel quilt paper. Crop and mat your photos, matting the final time with pastel quilt paper. Glue the quilt Punch-Out™ and journaling rectangle to the page. Arrange the photos, overlapping as shown. Finish with the matted saying Punch-Out™.

Pastel Quilt Patterned Paper: *Paper Pizazz™ Baby* by Hot Off The Press

Quilt Punch-Out™: *Paper Pizazz™ Baby Punch-Outs™* by Hot Off The Press

Baby Saying Punch-Out™: *Paper Pizazz™ Sayings Punch-Outs™* by Hot Off The Press

Scissors: Colonial and Majestic Paper Edgers by Fiskars®, Inc.

Page Designer: Katie Hacker for Hot Off The Press

Great looking pages don't have to take long. Mat your different shaped photos on light blue paper. Arrange them on the page adding a cutout and stickers to journal. Finish with light blue triangles and cutouts at the corners.

Sun & Moon Patterned Paper: *Paper Pizazz™ Childhood* by Hot Off The Press
Stars and Sun Cutouts: *Paper Pizazz™ Childhood* by Hot Off The Press
Scissors: Ripple Paper Edgers by Fiskars®, Inc.
Alphabet Stickers: Frances Meyer Inc.®
Page Designer: Amberly Beck

A special picture deserves a special page! Double-mat the picture, then use cloud scissors to cut a 1" mat from cloud patterned paper. Use a round punch in each curve, then mat on yellow paper. Draw a ••—••— border just inside the punches. Glue the matted photo to the baby block paper. Use the pattern to cut three blocks. Draw and cut out simple letters and glue them to the blocks. Place a ribbon just below the picture and glue the blocks over it.

Baby Blocks Patterned Paper: *Paper Pizazz™ Baby* by Hot Off The Press
Cloud Patterned Paper: *Paper Pizazz™ Vacation* by Hot Off The Press
Scissors: Cloud and Scallop Paper Edgers Fiskars®, Inc.
1/8" Round Punch: McGill, Inc.
1/4" wide Blue Grosgrain Self-Adhesive Ribbon: Memory Book Ribbon by C.M. Offray & Son, Inc.
Page Designer: Becky Goughnour for Hot Off The Press

Use double-sided foam mounting tape to add dimension to your page. Trim two sides of the pastel dots paper and glue it to a light purple sheet. Use white and light purple plain papers to triple-mat your photos. Press ¼" long pieces of foam tape around the edges of each Punch-Out™. Overlap some photos and fill any empty areas. Be sure to write on the announcement before mounting it on the foam tape.

Pastel Dots Patterned Paper: *Paper Pizazz™ Baby* by Hot Off The Press
Annoucement, Bear and Booties Punch-Outs™: *Paper Pizazz™ Baby Punch-Outs™* by Hot Off The Press
Scissors: Heartbeat Paper Edgers by Fiskars®, Inc.
Page Designer: Debbie Peterson

Punch the edges and corners of a ½" wide mat. Glue white paper under the border punches, then mat on a dark purple paper that brings out the colors of the photo. Place the matted photo on patterned paper and journal, using the same color pen as the dark mat.

Pink & White Patterned Paper: Paper Patch®
Corner Cutter: McGill, Inc.
Hearts Border Punch: McGill, Inc.
Purple Pen: ZIG® Writer by EK Success Ltd.
Page Designer: LeNae Gerig for Hot Off The Press

Punches add the charming gumdrops under the photos. Double-mat the photos, leaving 1" under the photos. Punch many different-colored ovals and trim the ends. Glue the gumdrops under the photos. Use stickers to journal and punch combinations to add other embellishments, such as the lollipops and wrapped candy.

Rainbow Sweets Patterned Paper: *Paper Pizazz™ Childhood* by Hot Off The Press
Scissors: Scallop by Family Treasures
Alphabet Stickers: Frances Meyer Inc.®
Bear Punch: Marvy® Uchida
Circle, Oval and Rectangle Punches: Family Treasures
Heart Punch: McGill, Inc.
Page Designer: Debbie Hewitt

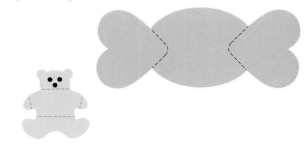

A simple background paper with colorful mats is an excellent start, but creative use of punches can make a good page spectacular. Punch many flowers and trim two petals off of each. Add a different-colored oval to the top of each flower and a stem below. Arrange the flowers so they curve inward, drawing your eye to the pictures. Punch black and red circles to create ladybugs. Cut the red circle in half and use the round punch to make four holes in each half. Arrange as though the bug is flying and add white eyes and black antennae.

Colorful Stripes Patterned Paper: *Paper Pizazz™ Birthday* by Hot Off The Press
Grass Patterned Paper: *Paper Pizazz™ Pets* by Hot Off The Press
Scissors: Mini Scallop and Scallop Paper Edgers by Fiskars®, Inc.
¹/₁₆" Round Punch: McGill, Inc.
Alphabet Stickers: Frances Meyer Inc.®
Circle, Flower and Oval Punches: Family Treasures
Page Designer: Debbie Hewitt

A 12"x12" page allows room for special effects. Trim an 8¹/₂"x11" sheet of patterned paper with scissors and glue in the center of the page. Trim your photos with a corner rounder then double-mat. Glue the die cut letters to the outside of the page. Draw simple stitches around one photo mat, the letters and the edge of the 8¹/₂"x11" sheet. Finish by adding the boot cutout to one corner and journaling on another.

Cowboy Patterned Paper: *Paper Pizazz™ Masculine Papers* by Hot Off The Press

Scissors: Deckle Paper Edgers by Fiskars®, Inc.

Boot Cutout: *Paper Pizazz™ Masculine Papers* by Hot Off The Press

Alphabet Die Cuts: Ellison® Craft & Design

Corner Cutter: Corner Rounder by Marvy® Uchida

Page Designer: LeNae Gerig for Hot Off The Press

Trim the map paper with decorative scissors and glue to the black paper. Cut some black strips and add them to the sides of the matted photos. Add small white rectangle punches on the black areas to give the impression of a road. Place punched cars on either side of the road and combine rectangle and circle punches to make traffic signals.

Road Map Patterned Paper: *Paper Pizazz™ Vacation* by Hot Off The Press

Scissors: Stamp Paper Edgers by Fiskars®, Inc.

Car, Circle and Rectangle Punches: Family Treasures

Small Rectangle Punch: McGill, Inc.

Page Designer: Debbie Hewitt

Creating a baby album

Using the ideas and techniques on the previous pages, these pages demonstrate how to create an album using similar colors, complimentary pages and different photos from different milestones in your baby's life.

Remember that album pages face each other. Use the same papers and elements on each page, such as the foot punches and offset matting. Journaling "Molly" in different styles at the top of each page allows the pages to have slightly different looks while still harmonizing. Journaling on each offset mat allows room to comment on each photo.

Footprint and Yellow & White Dot Patterned Papers: Paper Patch®
Scissors: Antique by Family Treasures
Corner Cutter: Corner Rounder by Marvy® Uchida
Blue, Red and White Pens: ZIG® Writer by EK Success Ltd.
Foot Punch: Marvy® Uchida
Page Designer: Becky Goughnour for Hot Off The Press

Double-mat a portrait cropped with decorative scissors, then mat on a patterned paper trimmed in a rectangle. Mat once more, using different scissors, before gluing to the center of a patterned sheet. Use Punch-Outs™ to quickly and easily support the page theme. Journal by cutting out bubble letters drawn on patterned paper. Glue them to a matted oval, adding lettering underneath.

Blue Chalk and Pink & Blue Plaid Patterned Papers: *Paper Pizazz™ Light Great Backgrounds* by Hot Off The Press
Moon and Star Punch-Outs™: *Paper Pizazz™ Baby Punch-Outs™* by Hot Off The Press
Scissors: Cloud and Ripple Paper Edgers by Fiskars®, Inc.
Blue and Red Pens: ZIG® Writer by EK Success Ltd.
Page Designer: Becky Goughnour for Hot Off The Press

Molly's quilt pictures provide the inspiration for this page. Mat a 5"x8" piece of blue paper with cream. Repeat with pink. Draw a ••—••— border around the inside of the blue and pink papers. Glue to the center of a quilt sheet. Place the matted photos on the matted blue sheet. Punch blue, cream and pink hearts and draw simple stitching around the outside of each. Use the punches to frame the mat. Journal at the top of the page.

Irish Chain Quilt Patterned Paper: *Paper Pizazz™ Country* by Hot Off The Press

Scissors: Scallop Paper Edgers by Fiskars®, Inc.

Heart Punches: Marvy® Uchida

Black Pens: ZIG® Calligraphy and Writer by EK Success Ltd.

Page Designer: LeNae Gerig for Hot Off The Press

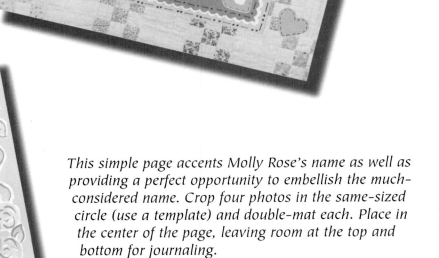

This simple page accents Molly Rose's name as well as providing a perfect opportunity to embellish the much-considered name. Crop four photos in the same-sized circle (use a template) and double-mat each. Place in the center of the page, leaving room at the top and bottom for journaling.

Rose Trellis Patterned Paper: Frances Meyer Inc.®

Scissors: Cloud Paper Edgers by Fiskars®, Inc.

Green Pen: ZIG® Writer by EK Success Ltd.

Page Designer: LeNae Gerig for Hot Off The Press

Die cuts provide an excellent place to journal. List the important details on the large bunny, then add the year on the eggs. Attach the ribbon to the top and bottom of the page. Glue the matted bunny, eggs and photos overlapped as shown.

Gingham Check, Polka Dot and Plaid Patterned Papers: Paper Patch®

Bunny and Egg Die Cuts: Ellison® Craft & Design

Purple Pen: ZIG® Writer by EK Success Ltd.

Self-Adhesive Ribbon: Memory Book Ribbon by C.M. Offray & Son, Inc.

Page Designer: LeNae Gerig for Hot Off The Press

Easily create matching pages by carefully cutting out the center of the hydrangea paper in a rounded rectangle. Place the rectangle on one sheet of purple sponged paper and the frame on another sheet. Double-mat a Punch-Out™ to introduce the page theme and journal around it to provide the details. Create a swirl on each side, to add a touch of elegance. Mat the photos on bright papers to flatter the Punch-Out™ and provide color. Reinforce the theme with other Punch-Outs™.

Hydrangea and Purple Sponged Patterned Papers: *Paper Pizazz™ Pretty Papers* by Hot Off The Press

Vacation, Camera and Suitcase Punch-Outs™: *Paper Pizazz™ Vacation Punch-Outs™* by Hot Off The Press

Page Designer: LeNae Gerig for Hot Off The Press

Cut four ¹/₂"x11" strips out of the dots on purple paper. Mat each on a different color paper and trim with decorative scissors. Cut a 6³/₄"x9" piece of confetti paper and glue it to the center of a dots on purple page. Lay the matted strips over the confetti paper to hide the edges. Use a template to crop your photos and mat them adding a balloon tie on each. Mat again on dots on purple paper and glue as shown, adding a matted journal note in one corner.

Confetti Patterned Paper: *Paper Pizazz™ Birthday* by Hot Off The Press
Dots on Purple Patterned Paper: *Paper Pizazz™ Child's Play* by Hot Off The Press
Scissors: Jigsaw Paper Edgers by Fiskars®, Inc.
Heart Punch: Marvy® Uchida
Heart Template: Extra Special Products
¹/₈" wide **Purple Satin Self-Adhesive Ribbon:** Memory Book Ribbon by C.M. Offray & Son, Inc.
Page Designer: Katie Hacker for Hot Off The Press

This page ends the album well; Molly is obviously older than when the album started. A new album could focus on her toddler years. Trim the duckie paper to 7¹/₂"x10", mat on blue and glue to one side of a yellow sheet. Use the pattern on page 139 to draw and cut out the tub. Crop two photos in a circle and double-mat. Cut around the outline of another photo. Place this photo in the tub. Use stickers and duckie cutouts to complete the scene.

Duckies Patterned Paper: *Paper Pizazz™ Baby* by Hot Off The Press
Rubber Duckie Cutouts: *Paper Pizazz™ Baby* by Hot Off The Press
Scissors: Cloud and Scallop Paper Edgers by Fiskars®, Inc.
Bubble Stickers: Frances Meyer Inc.®
Page Designer: Katie Hacker for Hot Off The Press

Let's play dress up

Garrett on the Go!

eat my dust!

Derek's First Suit - look at the grin!

Our Bouncing Baby Boys

40

Childhood

Our childhood memories are so important to us, it makes sense to design album pages that reflect our reverence of the years gone past. It's important to include daily play activities (see the top of page 46) as well as childhood milestones (see the bottom of page 43). This chapters exhibits ideas and techniques that we can use to create an album as unique as the child within.

Making a collage of closely cropped photos not only depicts the event, but can also do a great job of capturing the child's personality (see the tops of pages 43, 53 and 57). Backed by patterned paper and decorated with stickers and punches, these album pages become exceptional!

For the innovative scrapbooker, use punches to create unique "patterned" paper. Both examples on page 45 use punches to decorate the background. At the bottom of page 48, patterned paper is used to design flower blossom photo frames. At the top of page 52, a woven border capped with images cut from patterned paper frames the page.

Throughout this chapter, we offer ideas and useful techniques to let the exuberance of childhood shine in our memory albums. Ballerina background paper is a perfect spin-off of the little girl's ballet costume (bottom of page 42). A creative inclusion is the "Favorite Things" list shown at the bottom of page 57. Ribbon borders and flowers create a feminine feel in both examples on page 56 and at the top of page 57.

Of course, childhood pages don't have to portray only "children." They also can show off the "child" within each of us as shown at the tops of pages 44, 47 and 56, and at the bottom of page 51.

The border for this section was created using
Stamp Paper Edgers by Fiskars®, Inc.

Cut seven 12" lengths of ribbon, cutting on the same portion of the pattern each time. Arrange diagonally on a plain sheet of 12"x12" paper, leaving $^1/_2$" between each ribbon length. Glue the matted photos to the page.

Textured Paper: Hygloss Products, Inc.
Scissors: Jumbo Deckle by Family Treasures
Self-Adhesive Ribbon: Memory Book Ribbon
    by C.M. Offray & Son, Inc.
Page Designer: Carla Spence for C.M. Offray
    & Son, Inc.

Use deckle scissors to trim a sheet of ballerina paper to 7"x9$^1/_2$". Cut off the left corner. Glue to a sheet of white paper. Trim the white paper to 8"x10$^1/_2$" with the seagull scissors. Cut off the left corner as shown, using the deckle scissors. Use the round punch to make a hole under each small scallop of the white mat. Draw "stitches" along the long scallops. Glue to a pink page as shown, then mat each photo in a similar style. Place stickers along the left corner for journaling.

Ballerina Patterned Paper: *Paper Pizazz*™
    Little Charmers by Hot Off The Press
Scissors: Deckle and Seagull Paper Edgers
    by Fiskars®, Inc.
$^1/_8$" **Round Punch:** McGill, Inc.
Alphabet and Number Stickers: Frances
    Meyer Inc.®
Page Designer: Debbie Peterson

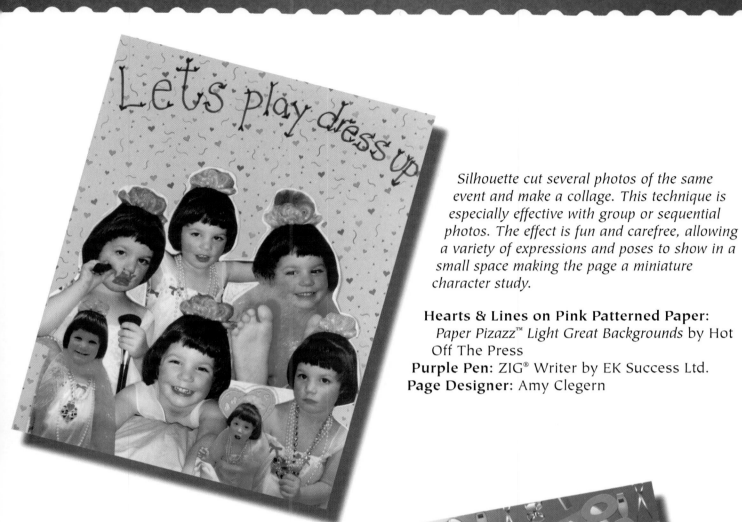

Let's play dress up

Silhouette cut several photos of the same event and make a collage. This technique is especially effective with group or sequential photos. The effect is fun and carefree, allowing a variety of expressions and poses to show in a small space making the page a miniature character study.

Hearts & Lines on Pink Patterned Paper: *Paper Pizazz™ Light Great Backgrounds* by Hot Off The Press
Purple Pen: ZIG® Writer by EK Success Ltd.
Page Designer: Amy Clegern

Select a background paper that matches the photos' theme, then glue the matted photos and die cut scissors to the page. Cut the striped paper to 2¹/₂"x4¹/₂" for the barbershop pole and top it with ¹/₂" strips of plain blue paper. Journal on white and mat once, then place on the pole. Glue the pole to the bottom right corner.

Barbershop Patterned Paper: *Paper Pizazz™ Book of Firsts* by Hot Off The Press
Red & White Stripes Patterned Paper: *Paper Pizazz™ Christmas* by Hot Off The Press
Scissors Die Cut: Canson® Self Adhesive Die Cut
Page Designer: LeNae Gerig for Hot Off The Press

June 1997
Hair cut Day for Caleb and Joseph

When you are not sure what to do with a set of photos, choose a background paper that will provide a theme! The journaling on this page links the photos to the blue jeans paper and makes the page flow. Matting with bright red sets off the photos and creates a rich note of color. Add a final touch with subtle journaling under each picture.

Blue Jeans Patterned Paper: *Paper Pizazz™ Teen Years* by Hot Off The Press
Page Designer: Allison Myers for Memory Lane

Trim a piece of patterned paper and place it on a sheet with a similar or coordinating pattern. Mat the photos on black, leaving a wide allowance. Punch the edges to imitate film. Cut out the filmstrip pattern from black paper. Use rectangle, square and triangle punches to make the pattern into a film strip. (Film strip pattern on page 142.)

Blue Corrugated and Red Corrugated Patterned Papers: *Paper Pizazz™ Country* by Hot Off The Press
Scissors: Leaf Paper Edgers by Fiskars®, Inc.
Square, Triangle and Rectangle Punches: McGill, Inc.
Page Designer: Debbie Hewitt

Glue three photos to a piece of patterned paper. Mat as one image and glue to another sheet. To make the pearl necklaces, use the ¼" round punch and glue many white circles in trails around the page, adding a white heart occasionally. To create the mirrors, cut out several pink ovals using the decorative scissors and combine with rectangle and oval punches. Punch pink lips and glue in the empty areas. Cut out the patterns and use to journal.

Lines & Hearts on Pink Patterned Paper:
   Paper Pizazz™ Light Great Backgrounds by Hot Off The Press
Metallic Silver Paper: Hygloss Products, Inc.
Scissors: Scallop by Family Treasures
¼" Round Punch: McGill, Inc.
Heart, Lips, Oval and Rectangle Punches: Family Treasures
Pink Pen: ZIG® Writer by EK Success Ltd.
Page Designer: Debbie Hewitt

Everyday photos are glued to white paper and cut out with a ½" border. Punch the mat with the mini flower punch, then mat on yellow. Use the ⅛" round punch for the center of each flower. Mat on brown, then glue the matted photos on denim paper. Punch many yellow suns and ¼" brown circles. Make many 1/16" punches in the largest circles. Glue the brown circles to the appropriate size of sunflowers, then to the page, filling empty areas. Use stickers to journal the name at the top of the page.

Denim Patterned Paper: *Paper Pizazz™ Country* by Hot Off The Press
1/16", ⅛" and ¼" Round Punches: McGill, Inc.
Alphabet Stickers: Making Memories™
Circle and Medium Sun Punches: Family Treasures
Long Reach Sun Punch: McGill, Inc.
Mini Flower Punch: All Night Media®, Inc.
Page Designer: Debbie Hewitt

A simple trick for an interesting page is to mat one photo, then silhouette two others. Place the matted photo in the center of the page and arrange the silhouetted photos on each side, slightly overlapping the matted photo. This creates a variety of shapes, as well as giving an active feeling to the page. Finish the page with punched swirls that pick up a mat color. Notice the unique use of turning a swirl into the letter "e" in Keaton's name.

Stripe Patterned Paper: Paper Patch®
Brown Pen: ZIG® Writer by EK Success Ltd.
Swirl Punch: All Night Media®, Inc.
Page Designer: Allison Myers for Memory Lane

© & ™ Ellison® Craft & Design

Die cuts are a great shortcut! Frame your photo in a die cut mat, then place die cut blocks at the bottom of the page. Punch out the center of another set of colored paper die cut blocks and glue over the first set. Use a lettering template to cut out letters in the same colors as the block frames and glue to the center of the blocks.

Block and Frame Die Cuts: Ellison® Craft & Design
Lettering Template: Block Lettering Tracer by Pebbles in My Pocket
Page Designer: Amber Blakesley for Paper Hearts

Create a quilted background sheet by cutting an 8¹/₂" square out of the blue lines & dots paper. Glue at an angle to the center of a plain blue sheet. Glue a 2" square of red lines & dots paper to each corner of the plain paper. Crop the photos with decorative scissors. Mat as shown, cutting the rampart edge at the top of each mat. Mat one red-matted and one yellow-matted photo on its opposite mat color. Glue to the page as shown. Duplicate the cutting shapes for the journaling papers.

Lines & Dots Patterned Paper: *Paper Pizazz™ Birthday* by Hot Off The Press
Red Lines & Dots Patterned Paper: *Paper Pizazz™ Bright Great Backgrounds* by Hot Off The Press
Scissors: Jigsaw Paper Edgers by Fiskars®, Inc.
Page Designer: Anne-Marie Spencer for Hot Off The Press

Coordinate your scrapbook by placing portraits on adjoining pages. Place a full-body shot on one page and a close-up on another. Run die cuts along the bottom to bring the pages together, as was done with this train. (Remaining train patterns on page 140. Frame pattern on page 139.)

Bear and Medium Heart Punches: Marvy® Uchida
Train, Popcorn, Button, Star and Frame Die Cuts: Ellison® Craft & Design
Page Designer: Amber Blakesley for Paper Hearts

When you don't have enough photos to fill up a page, look around for accents. These stickers emphasize the photos' theme and create a fun border. Place the large stickers on the corners and sides, then use the ruler to draw wavy lines to the sides. Add small stickers along the lines to connect the larger images. Notice the journaling along a cut oval photo.

Teal Stars Patterned Paper: *Paper Pizazz™ Bright Great Backgrounds* by Hot Off The Press
Scissors: Deckle Paper Edgers by Fiskars®, Inc.
Ruler Template: Déjà Views™ by C-Thru® Ruler Co.
Stickers: Provo Craft®
Page Designer: Debbie Peterson

Glue a ¹/₂" patterned strip trimmed with decorative scissors to each side of a plain sheet. Use the pattern to cut three large flowers out of the same patterned paper and three small flowers out of plain paper. Cut four leaves and three ³/₈" wide strips for stems. Arrange on the page as shown, then use a template to crop your photos into 2¹/₄" circles. Glue one to the center of each flower. Draw stitches around the outside of the leaves and small flowers.

Brown & Gold Swirl Patterned Paper: *Paper Pizazz™ Black & White Photos* by Hot Off The Press
Scissors: Mini Pinking Paper Edgers by Fiskars®, Inc.
Page Designer: Debbie Peterson

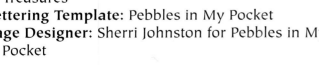

Trim the grass paper to 7½"x10½" and glue to the center of a plain piece of brown paper. Double mat the photos and Punch-Out™, then arrange on the grass paper. Use a ruler to create the fence out of barnwood paper and place at the bottom of each picture. Add stickers at the bottom of each fence and scatter some around the page to connect the page elements. Journal in the empty areas.

Barnwood Patterned Paper: *Paper Pizazz™ Country* by Hot Off The Press
Grass Patterned Paper: *Paper Pizazz™ Pets* by Hot Off The Press
Spring Fever Punch-Out™: *Paper Pizazz™ Sayings Punch-Outs™* by Hot Off The Press
Scissors: Dragon-Back and Mini-Pinking Paper Edgers by Fiskars®, Inc.
Fence Ruler: Déjà Views™ by C-Thru® Ruler Co.
Flower Stickers: ©Mrs. Grossman's Paper Co.
Page Designer: Debbie Peterson

It isn't necessary to crop photos in order to have a beautiful page. Cut a 7"x10½" piece of green paper and place two photos evenly spaced on it. Place this in the center of a green plaid piece of paper. Punch seven white flowers and seven yellow circles. Glue one circle in the center of each flower, then cluster three flowers at the top right and lower left corners of the page. Use the lettering template to cut a name out of patterned paper. Glue the letters between the photos, placing the remaining flower among the letters.

Green Plaid Patterned Papers: Northern Spy
¼" **Round and Large Flower Punches:** Family Treasures
Lettering Template: Pebbles in My Pocket
Page Designer: Sherri Johnston for Pebbles in My Pocket

Draw attention to your photos by creating a scene. Double mat the photos, then mat three 2³/₈"x3" white rectangles on black. Draw a dashed border around each white rectangle, write seeds in the lower center, then use punches to make the various fruits and vegetables. Make tomatoes using the balloon and small sun punches. Create peas with scallop scissors and strawberries using the heart, large sun cut in half and round punches. Glue the seed packets to ¹/₄" wide "posts." Cut free form soil and glue to the bottom of the patterned paper. Glue the other pieces as shown.

White Dot on Green Patterned Paper: *Paper Pizazz™ Christmas* by Hot Off The Press
Scissors: Mini Pinking Paper Edgers by Fiskars®, Inc.
Scissors: Scallop by Family Treasures
¹/₄" and ¹/₁₆" Round Punches: McGill, Inc.
Balloon, Large Sun and Rectangle Punches: Family Treasures
Heart and Small Sun Punches: McGill, Inc.
Page Designer: Debbie Hewitt

The easiest way to make an attractive page is to select a paper and coordinating Punch-Outs™ to match the theme of your photos. The photos on this page pick up the colors and the shape of the Ouch! Punch-Out™, drawing the eye between the photos and other page elements.

Bandage Patterned Paper: *Paper Pizazz™ Childhood* by Hot Off The Press
Bandage Punch-Outs™: *Paper Pizazz™ Kids Punch-Outs™* by Hot Off The Press
Scissors: Peaks Paper Edgers by Fiskars®, Inc.
Page Designer: Amberly Beck

Dress-up a plain page with varying matting techniques and stickers! Combine mat shapes and sizes when matting. One circle photo is matted on a square while another is double offset matted. Note the heart punches in the corners of the square mat. Use stickers at the corners of a mat or to frame journaling. Place them at the corner of a mat to soften the edge and connect the page elements. Note how the stickers on this page strengthen the theme as well as add color.

Scissors: Dragon-back, Mini-Scallop and
  Zipper Paper Edgers by Fiskars®, Inc.
Stickers: ©Mrs. Grossman's Paper Co.
Page Designer: Bridgette Server for
  Memories & More™

Turn many small photos into a larger arrangement by using a template to cut them into diamonds. Arrange the cropped photos on a denim cube cut with a hexagon template. Make three cubes, then arrange on a 7"x10" trimmed white page glued to a denim sheet. Add stickers above and below each cube, softening the edges and emphasizing the nature theme. Journal in the empty areas.

Denim Patterned Paper: *Paper Pizazz™ Country* by Hot Off The Press
Scissors: Aztec Paper Edgers by Fiskars®, Inc.
Diamond Template: Extra Special Products
Stickers: ©Mrs. Grossman's Paper Co.
Page Designer: Debbie Peterson

The Peterson Family

• Camping & Hiking at Lake Wallowa

•Dad•Mom•
•Amberly•Tara•
•Derek•Megan•
•Chad•

*Use the ruler template to draw four white and four ¹/₄"
wide blue wavy paper strips. Cut out and weave them
together, then glue one to each edge of the page. Place a
¹/₂" circle cut with decorative scissors in each corner to
connect the strips and hide the edges. Cut the small bears
and bees from the patterned paper and glue to the woven
strips. Glue the Punch-Out™, matted journaling and
matted photos to the inner page as shown.*

Bear & Bees Patterned Paper: *Paper Pizazz™ Childhood*
by Hot Off The Press
Honey Bear Punch-Out™: *Paper Pizazz™ Kids Punch-
Outs™* by Hot Off The Press
Scissors: Deckle and Mini-Scallop Paper Edgers by
Fiskars®, Inc.
Ruler: Déjà Views™ by C-Thru® Ruler Co.
Page Designer: Debbie Peterson

Bear & Bees from
Paper Pizazz™
Childhood

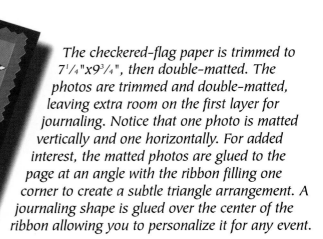

*The checkered-flag paper is trimmed to
7¹/₄"x9³/₄", then double-matted. The
photos are trimmed and double-matted,
leaving extra room on the first layer for
journaling. Notice that one photo is matted
vertically and one horizontally. For added
interest, the matted photos are glued to the
page at an angle with the ribbon filling one
corner to create a subtle triangle arrangement. A
journaling shape is glued over the center of the
ribbon allowing you to personalize it for any event.*

Checkered-Flag Patterned Paper: *Paper
Pizazz™ Masculine Papers* by Hot Off The
Press
Ribbon Cutout: *Paper Pizazz™ Pets* by Hot Off
The Press
Scissors: Peaks Paper Edgers by Fiskars®, Inc.
Page Designer: Debbie Peterson

Use decorative scissors to trim a large sheet to 10¾"x11¼" and center on a 12"x12" sheet. Double mat the photos, using decorative scissors with plain scissors on the silhouetted photos. Be sure to use bright matting paper to accent the pattered paper.

Colorful Stripes and Hearts, Coils, Stars Patterned Papers: *Paper Pizazz™ Childhood Memories* by Hot Off The Press
Scissors: Ripply by McGill, Inc.
Alphabet Stickers: Making Memories™
Page Designer: LeNae Gerig for Hot Off The Press

Use geometrically shaped stickers to create a border around the page, then crop and mat the photos into similar shapes. Draw simple stitches around the outside of each mat. Notice the photo matted on the triangle is silhouetted, rather than following the shape of the mat. Journal on a green circle and slip under the edge of one photo.

Black Pen: ZIG® Writer by EK Success Ltd.
Stickers: ©Mrs. Grossman's Paper Co.
Template: Extra Special Products
Page Designer: Allison Myers for Memory Lane

Favorite photos can be given a theme with the right stickers and journaling. Start with black and white check paper and place a slightly trimmed piece of gold over it. Double-mat one photo in the same manner as the journaling and mat two on red. Place the red-matted photos on opposite sides of the double-matted photo. This connects the two photos and keeps the eye moving to the different elements. Stickers which emphasize the car toy and journaling finish the page.

Black & White Check and Gingham Patterned Papers: Paper Patch®
Stickers: Stickopotamus™ by EK Success Ltd.
Page Designer: Ann Smith for Memory Lane

© & ™ Ellison® Craft & Design

Three large photos don't fit on a page. Instead of fighting it, go with the flow! Overlapping is a wonderful visual trick for adding interest. Don't be afraid to break borders or trim corners from mats. This arrangement leaves the page corners open for journaling and decoration!

Blue & White Stripe Patterned Paper: Provo Craft®
Wood Patterned Paper: Memory Lane
Silver Pen: Marvy® Uchida Gel Roller
Stickers: ©Mrs. Grossman's Paper Co.
Wrench Die Cut: Ellison® Craft & Design
Page Designer: Ann Smith for Memory Lane

It isn't necessary to have photos on every page in your album. Cut two pieces of 8³/₈"x10¹/₂" white paper. Round two edges of each with corner rounders. Use a die cut frame to mat your photo on one page, then cut four ⁷/₈" strips and four 1¹/₄" strips of plain paper. Place the thinner strips diagonally on the portrait page. Place the thicker strips horizontally on the adjoining page. Use the lettering template to cut a name out of black paper. (Frame pattern on page 139.)

Corner Cutter: Corner Rounder by Marvy® Uchida
Frame Die Cut: Ellison® Craft & Design
Lettering Template: Pebbles in My Pocket
Page Designer: Amber Blakesley for Paper Hearts

Photos can be matted using any combination of plain and decorative scissors. The photos on this page are matted in two different styles, then placed on the page. The extra strips from trimming the mats are glued to the top and bottom. A block Punch-Out™ is glue to the center and another is cut apart, then glued to three different corners, connecting the page areas.

Block Punch-Outs™: *Paper Pizazz™ Kids Punch-Outs™* by Hot Off The Press
Hands Patterned Paper: *Paper Pizazz™ Childhood* by Hot Off The Press
Scissors: Peaks Paper Edgers by Fiskars®, Inc.
Page Designer: Amberly Beck

Pages don't have to look exactly alike to go together. Use a similar element on each page in your album, such as the dotted ribbon on this page and the next two. Center a ⅝"x12" length of dotted ribbon on a 1¼"x12" length of blue satin ribbon. Glue to one side of the page. Trim the pink and white ribbon at a 45° angle and use it to frame the photos. Before gluing, cut a blue mat and place it under the picture and ribbon. For an elegant final touch, draw a flower vine and glue ribbon roses over the pattern.

⅝" **wide Pink & White Dotted and 1" wide Blue Satin Ribbon:** Self-Adhesive Memory Book Ribbon by C.M. Offray & Son, Inc.
¾"–1" **wide Ribbon Roses:** C.M. Offray & Son, Inc.
Colored Pencils: Berol Krismacolor
Scissors: Jumbo Deckle by Family Treasures
Page Designer: Carla Spence for C.M. Offray & Son, Inc.

Glue 1½" strips of ribbon around the page edges to create the look of a woven border. To create a bow, glue two 3" loops on top of a 3" and 4" length of ribbon. Glue a ribbon rose to the center. Mat the photos, place on the page and add ribbon roses below them.

⅝" **wide Pink & White Dotted Ribbon:** Self-Adhesive Memory Book Ribbon by C.M. Offray & Son, Inc.
½"–1" **wide Ribbon Roses:** C.M. Offray & Son, Inc.
Scissors: Deckle Paper Edgers by Fiskars®, Inc.
Page Designer: Carla Spence for C.M. Offray & Son, Inc.

Center three 12" lengths of dotted ribbon over slightly wider light blue ribbon and glue to the page as shown. Cut many photos with a heart template and mat with pink or blue. Add shoestring ribbon bows to the picture tops and glue to the page. Use a template to cut a small pink heart and journal on it. Mat on blue and glue to the page top.

⁵⁄₈" wide Pink & White Dotted Ribbon: Self-Adhesive Memory Book Ribbon by C.M. Offray & Son, Inc.

Ribbon Bows: C.M. Offray & Son, Inc.

Heart Template: Extra Special Products

Scissors: Deckle Paper Edgers by Fiskars®, Inc.

Page Designer: Carla Spence for C.M. Offray & Son, Inc.

If a photo could speak, it would tell you the person's history. Since it can't, let your page do the talking. Create a "Favorite Things" form on acid-free paper and let your child fill it out with an acid-free pen. Mat it with a photo and glue to the page. Use die cuts to announce the name and make your own comments in the empty areas.

Colorful Dots Patterned Paper: *Paper Pizazz*™ *School Days* by Hot Off The Press

Crayon Font Computer Typeface: D.J. Inkers™ Fontastic

Letter Die Cuts: Ellison® Craft & Design

Page Designer: Launa Naylor for Pebbles in My Pocket

School, Sports & Teens

School years seem to produce more photos than report cards! This chapter provides enough ideas to display them all, whether pre-school, teen or sporting activities. Photos of children during every school-age phase— from her pre-kindergarten doctor's visit at the bottom of page 61, to their spring break vacation shown at the top of page 69— look great, especially when displayed using the ideas shown here!

Plain papers come in a wide assortment to match any school color combination, like the gold and maroon of the Vikings at the top of page 65. Patterned papers can adorn any page, such as the ladybugs chosen for the school play photos shown at the top of page 60. While patterned papers such as paint splats or handprints may seem juvenile, you'll find them very appropriate when used as mats for these photos of a paintball party at the bottom of page 67, or the back-to-school finger painting party page at the bottom of page 69.

The page at the top of page 65 exhibits one idea for displaying your school's mascot with a die cut. Or, you can feature a senior year portrait with mortar board stickers or a rolled-up diploma die cut as shown on pages 60 and 64. And we loved the idea at the top of page 61 of creating a two-page spread to include the artwork made in school. Just be sure to photocopy the originals onto acid-free paper!

Crop the photo and mat once. Trace the flower patterns, cut out and glue to the page. Cut out the leaves and glue under the flowers. Glue the matted photos to the flower centers. Frame opposite page corners with the same paper used for the flowers. Use circle and oval templates to create ladybug bodies. Punch the red circles with the round punches. Glue the ladybugs in the empty areas. Use a ruler to draw stitches and journaling along wavy lines to connect the elements and frame the page. (Flower mat and leaf patterns on page 141.)

Cream Handmade Patterned Paper: *Paper Pizazz™ Handmade Papers* by Hot Off The Press
Scissors: Deckle Paper Edgers by Fiskars®, Inc.
$1/8$" **Round Punch:** McGill, Inc.
$1/4$" **Round Punch:** McGill, Inc.
$1/2$" **Round Punch:** Marvy® Uchida
Circle and Oval Templates: Déjà Views™ by C-Thru® Ruler Co.
Ruler Template: Déjà Views™ by C-Thru® Ruler Co.
Page Designer: Debbie Peterson

This page has two patterned papers pieced together to make a 12"x12" background. A sticker borderline is used to hide the seams of the graduation patterned papers. The matted photo is glued slightly off-center. The die cut and stickers draw the eye to the photo, keeping the eye moving to the different elements. (Diploma pattern on page 139.)

Graduation Patterned Paper: *Paper Pizazz™ School Days* by Hot Off The Press
Red Tartan Patterned Paper: *Paper Pizazz™ Christmas* by Hot Off The Press
Design Line: ©Mrs. Grossman's Paper Co.
Diploma Die Cut: Ellison® Craft & Design
Mortar Board and Alphabet Stickers: ©Mrs. Grossman's Paper Co.
Page Designer: Stephanie Taylor

Patterned paper is often used as a background paper, but here it is cut into letters and used to mat the drawings. Outline each letter with a black pen. Color photocopy childhood drawings onto acid-free paper then mat. Journal near each drawing.

Hands Patterned Paper:
  Paper Pizazz™ *Childhood* by Hot Off The Press
Paintbrush and Splat Die Cuts: Pebbles in My Pocket
Lettering Template: Pebbles in My Pocket
Page Designer: Launa Naylor for Pebbles in My Pocket

This quick and easy page is embellished to echo the theme of a visit to the doctor. The angled photos add to the fun. After double-matting and overlapping the photos onto the page, add a journaled die cut to one side of the photos. Draw a —||—|| border around the page and photos. Journal above one photo.

Apple Plaid Patterned Paper: Paper Patch®
Apple Die Cut: Ellison® Craft & Design
Page Designer: Sherri Johnston for Pebbles in My Pocket

© & ™ Ellison® Craft & Design

When using plain papers, add variety to the page with lettering and die cuts. Glue an asymmetrical blue strip in the center of a white page (or glue a white strip on the top and bottom of a blue page). Double-mat the photos and place them on opposite corners. Journal in the lower left corner. Add a die cut and lettering to opposite corners to balance the page.

Metallic Gold Paper: *Paper Pizazz™ Metallic Papers* by Hot Off The Press
Lettering Template: Pebbles in My Pocket
Mortar Board Die Cut: Ellison® Craft & Design
Page Designer: Erika Clayton for Pebbles in My Pocket

April 1993
Rob received
his Bachelor's
Degree in
Civil Engineering

Many die cuts are scored to provide guides for added detailing. On this page, cut four crayons from brightly colored papers. Cut four crayons each from black and white paper. Cut the tips and ends from the black and white crayons to create "labels." Glue the white labels to the center of the colored crayons. Cut half circles from the top of the black labels and glue them over the white. Write the crayon color in each label. This technique works well when the die cuts accent the photo's theme or the patterned paper.

Chad William Naylor   Age 3½

Crayons Patterned Paper: *Paper Pizazz™ Childhood* by Hot Off The Press
Crayon Die Cut: Ellison® Craft & Design
Page Designer: Launa Naylor for Pebbles in My Pocket

My First Day of Pre-School
-1983-

I was so excited for my first day of Pre-School that I wore one of my favorite "twirly dresses." I was 4 years old and attended Mrs. Carroll's on Metropolitan Way with my best friend Libby

Punched paper lace creates a nice border against a dark paper. Glue a 4" wide white paper strip to a 5" wide dark blue strip. Glue paper lace extending ¹/₂" above and below the dark blue paper. Double-mat a photo and glue to one side of the white strip. Capture the feeling of the day by journaling on a piece of white paper and use punches to embellish. Add the date and page headline on the white strip. Place the matted white strip on the upper page and a matted photo and journaling on the bottom.

Corner Cutter: Corner Rounder by Marvy® Uchida
Heart Punch: Marvy® Uchida
Punched Paper Lace: Embossing Arts Co.
Scissors: Ripple Paper Edgers by Fiskars®, Inc.
Page Designer: Amber Blakesley for Paper Hearts

Die cuts set a theme, guide the eye and provide clear journaling space allowing the rest of the page to be filled with photos. Crop the photos, remembering to keep historical items like the piano. Mat on bright colors and glue to the page. Add smaller note stickers to fill any empty areas. (Piano pattern on page 142.)

Note and Piano Die Cuts: Ellison® Craft & Design
Note Stickers: ©Mrs. Grossman's Paper Co.
Scissors: Victorian Paper Edgers by Fiskars®, Inc.
Page Designer: Bridgette Server for Memories & More™

© & ™ Ellison® Craft & Design

My Piano Recital

School colors are a touch of memorabilia that can be included in school milestone photos. Cut a piece of white paper to 7³/₄"x10¹/₄". Glue to the center of a patterned sheet. Double-mat the photos, using the school's color scheme. Cut out the letters from plain orange paper and mat on black. Glue to the page as shown and add a mortar board sticker above the "G." Trim an orange template's shape into a ribbon to fit on a complete white template shape. Outline both pieces with a pen and journal under the photos.

Black and White Polka Dot Patterned Paper: Paper Patch®
Diploma Template: Pebbles in My Pocket
Lettering Template: Pebbles in My Pocket
Mortar Board Sticker: Suzy's Zoo®
Page Designer: Erika Clayton for Pebbles in My Pocket

Sports Pages

These pages contain ideas on how to make sports pages using team or individual photos. Also, there are ideas on cheerleading and sports parties.

Combining paper patterns can produce stunning effects. Remember to contrast dark and light patterns; the vertical stripes on this page are nicely broken by the dark polka dot paper. Add bright lettering and die cuts to provide color. Note how the die cuts seem to "move" across the page, drawing the eye immediately to the photo.

Green and White Stripe and Polka Dot Patterned Papers: Paper Patch®
Basketball and Letter Die Cuts: Ellison® Craft & Design
Page Designer: Karen McGavin for Pebbles in My Pocket

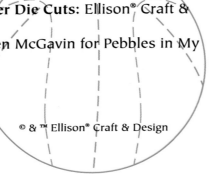

© & ™ Ellison® Craft & Design

Glue two ¼" wide gold strips and one ⅜" wide blue strip at the top and bottom of a page. Double-mat a photo in the same colors and glue off-center to the page. Offset double die cuts of the school mascot and student's jersey number to create a shadowed effect.

Eagle and Number Die Cuts: Ellison® Craft & Design
Page Designer: Karen McGavin for Pebbles in My Pocket

© & ™ Ellison® Craft & Design

With the busy background of these photos, the "star" can get lost. Cropping the photos can bring her back into focus. Be sure to use a variety of shapes when cropping to add a fun feeling to your page. The background paper lets the viewer know this is the football cheerleading squad. The matted journal letters cut from polka dot patterned paper displays the cheerleading squad's colors and completes the page.

Footballs Patterned Paper: Paper Pizazz™ Sports by Hot Off The Press
Yellow and White Polka Dot Patterned Paper: Paper Patch®
Lettering Template: Pebbles in My Pocket
Page Designer: Nancy Church for Pebbles in My Pocket

As long as it is acid-free, stationery can be used on your pages. Often stationery makes an excellent mat as it has large blank spaces perfect for photos. This striped mat, angled across a blue background, uses the team's colors and echoes the stripping of the uniforms. When cutting the journaling mat, wave your cuts to match the free form look of the striped stationery. Use a red pen to embellish the die cut baseball.

Baseball Die Cut: Ellison® Craft & Design
Lettering Template: Block Lettering Tracer by Pebbles in My Pocket
Stationery: Fitzgraphics, Inc.
Page Designer: Amber Blakesley for Paper Hearts

© & ™ Ellison® Craft & Design

Many people dislike their handwriting and hesitate to journal on their pages. Computers and quality printers have solved this problem! Type your comments in a paragraph, then cut out and mat. Place it on the page and you have comments to tell everyone what your page is about! The popcorn and bowl die cuts alert the viewer that this is a party rather than a game.

Football Field Patterned Paper: *Paper Pizazz*™ *Sports* by Hot Off The Press
Blue & White Gingham Patterned Paper: Paper Patch®
Football, Popcorn and Bowl Die Cuts: Ellison® Craft & Design
Page Designer: Nancy Church for Pebbles in My Pocket

© & ™ Ellison® Craft & Design

Match your background paper to your photos. Mat the photos on gray plain paper. Add stickers to connect the elements and fill the empty areas. When in doubt, remember that stickers don't always have to exactly match the page—they can indicate some element of the occasion that is not clear in the photos. (Golf club pattern on page 140.)

Golf Balls Patterned Paper: *Paper Pizazz™ Sports* by Hot Off The Press
Scissors: Deckle Paper Edgers by Fiskars®, Inc.
Stickers: ©Mrs. Grossman's Paper Co.
Page Designer: Debbie Peterson

Teen Activities
Teenagers have different experiences than children or adults, so sometimes a different type of page is needed. Select bright colors and remember to think youthful, but not childlike.

It's helpful to lay out your page before gluing the elements to the background paper. If you see your journaling will take up the entire page top, turn the sheet on its side to avoid blocky journaling. Mat on bright papers, cutting the mats in irregular, offset shapes as shown.

Lettering Stickers: Frances Meyer Inc.®
Splats Patterned Paper: *Paper Pizazz™ Childhood* by Hot Off The Press
Page Designer: Amy Clegern

This sophisticated page celebrates an important, independent accomplishment while still looking youthful and fun. Glue ¹/₂" wide strips to the top and bottom of the page. Mat each photo 2–5 times, varying mat widths, shapes, papers and colors. Use the pattern to cut out two ribbon tails. Outline each with a gold pen and glue under the medallion Punch-Out™. Glue the photos diagonally to the page, then add the ribbon.

Pink Amoeba Swirl, Purple Fire and Purple Satin Patterned Papers: *Paper Pizazz™ Bright Great Backgrounds* by Hot Off The Press
Pink Light Show Patterned Paper: *Paper Pizazz™ Light Great Backgrounds* by Hot Off The Press
Medallion Punch-Out™: *Paper Pizazz™ Kids Punch-Outs™* by Hot Off The Press
Scissors: Colonial Paper Edgers by Fiskars®, Inc.
Gold Pen: ZIG® Gel Writer by EK Success Ltd.
Corner Cutter: Round Corner Edger by Fiskars®, Inc.
Page Designer: Katie Hacker for Hot Off The Press

Cut a 2" wide pressed flower paper strip. Cut 1" wide slits ³/₄" apart in the center and weave a ³/₄" wide dark blue strip into them. Mat the flower strip on mauve then light blue. Glue to the blue handmade sheet. Mat each photo four times, using different papers and scissors. Double-mat the journaling and Punch-Out™. Glue matted corners at each right corner.

Blue Handmade and Pressed Flowers Patterned Papers: *Paper Pizazz™ Handmade Papers* by Hot Off The Press
Scissors: Colonial Paper Edgers by Fiskars®, Inc.
Sister Punch-Out™: *Paper Pizazz™ Sayings Punch-Outs™* by Hot Off The Press
Page Designer: Katie Hacker for Hot Off The Press

This 12"x12" album page has overlapping photos which provide a wonderful opportunity for some creative journaling with stickers. "Mexico City" bends to follow the shape of the photos and also guides the eye into the page. "Floating" bobs up toward the end as it follows the photos as "Gardens" trickles downward, like a waterfall. Notice the photos are matted with bright papers and seem to extend from one central photo.

Raindrops Patterned Paper:
   Paper Pizazz™ Childhood Memories by Hot Off The Press
Stickers: Frances Meyer Inc.®
Page Designer: Amy Clegern

Double-mat the photos on bright papers, using both plain and decorative scissors. Journal on a plain paper and cut out. Add individual comments on the mats of each photo. Arrange the elements on the lower half of the page before creating the headline. Draw simple lettering on patterned paper, outline with a thick black pen and cut out. Mat and arrange above the photos. Add hand punches around the page for fun.

Hands Patterned Paper: *Paper Pizazz™ Childhood* by Hot Off The Press
Scissors: Dragon-Back Paper Edgers by Fiskars®, Inc.
Hand Punch: Marvy® Uchida
Pen: ZIG® Writer by EK Success Ltd.
Page Designer: Katie Hacker for Hot Off The Press

Wedding

One would scarcely believe that wedding photos could be enhanced by anything; the day is so filled with warmth and love that the beauty shines through in even the portraits of a novice photographer. However, some simple techniques can make the most beautiful photos even more stunning. Throughout this chapter you will find many great examples of how to use corner cutters, stickers, die cuts and free-form penning to unveil the character behind each photo.

With such a wide array of soft romantic papers, the possible effects are endless! Lace papers come in many patterns and do a magnificent job of highlighting bridal veils such as is shown at the bottom of page 72. The patterned paper chosen as a background for the page at the bottom of page 74 is reminiscent of all that weddings imply: something old, something new; ages gone by and lives to be lived. The background paper and playful off-set matting is a wonderful combination to exhibit a page of Rachel's wedding at the bottom of page 77 that features not the groom, but the little boy!

Pages 80–83 show tips for creating a wedding album using the bride's colors. From engagement to honeymoon, we take you through one couple's activities and show you the techniques used to illustrate their day. Memory albums make such heartfelt gifts, whether for yourself or a friend. We know the tips in this chapter will help make your memory album the best it can be.

The border for this section was created using Seagull Paper Edgers by Fiskars®, Inc. and punches from McGill, Inc.

Add variety to your wedding album by creating some elaborate pages and some quick and easy entries. This page is gorgeous as well as easy to do. Mat the photos on purple moiré and antique laces paper. Glue to hydrangeas paper. Add antique laces corners, placing smaller, journaled purple moiré paper corners over them. Note how the flower and laces accent Jenny's gown and the outdoor setting.

Antique Laces, Hydrangeas and Purple Moiré Patterned Papers: *Paper Pizazz™ Pretty Papers* by Hot Off The Press
Scissors: Colonial Paper Edgers by Fiskars®, Inc.
Page Designers: LeNae Gerig and Becky Goughnour for Hot Off The Press

This page uses a different lace pattern for the background paper, creating a subtle variation of the previous page. The photos are double-matted on dark paper which brings out the light blue and green of the background paper. White punches soften the edges and connect the photos to the background. Both of these pages from Jenny's album are quick and easy.

Blue Handmade Patterned Paper: *Paper Pizazz™ Handmade Papers* by Hot Off The Press
Watercolor Lace Patterned Paper: Frances Meyer Inc.®
Calligraphy Pen: Pigma Callipen by Sakura
Flower Punch: Family Treasures
Page Designer: Becky Goughnour for Hot Off The Press

For the wide variety of photos on this page, it's important to have both formal and informal elements. The matted laser lace contrasts the casual swirl and embellishments. Scissors and double-matting produce a less formal but still elegant touch. Sometimes it's nice to have little or no journaling and let the photos speak for themselves.

Laser Lace: *Paper Pizazz™ Romantic Papers* by Hot Off The Press
Pansy Cutouts: *Paper Pizazz™ Embellishments* by Hot Off The Press
Purple Swirl Patterned Paper: *Paper Pizazz™ Very Pretty Papers* by Hot Off The Press
Scissors: Cloud Paper Edgers by Fiskars®, Inc.
Scissors: Mini Victorian by Family Treasures
Page Designer: LeNae Gerig for Hot Off The Press

Cut out the center of this lace page and glue it to the flower paper. Triple-mat the photos, alternately using dark and light papers trimmed with plain and decorative scissors. Glue the matted photos to the page, overlapping as shown. Add journaling in the empty areas. Notice how one journaling box curves to follow the line of the photo.

Lace and Stylized Flowers Patterned Papers: Frances Meyer Inc.®
Calligraphy Pen: Pigma Callipen by Sakura
Scissors: Victorian Paper Edgers by Fiskars®, Inc.
Page Designer: Becky Goughnour for Hot Off The Press

Our
Wedding Day
12/05/92

Many wedding photos are larger than normal, but three small snapshots can work on a page with some creative embellishments. Mat the photos and place stickers around them. Draw wavy lines on the stickers with a gold pen. Trim a plain piece of paper and use the large round punch in the curves of the scissors' design. Use a smaller round punch between each large punch, varying the placement to achieve a wavy effect. Place gold paper under the punched piece, trimming the gold so it doesn't extend beyond the paper. Mat on burgundy paper, then arrange the matted photos and die cuts as shown before journaling.

Metallic Gold Paper: Hygloss Products, Inc.
Scissors: Victorian Paper Edgers by Fiskars®, Inc.
$1/16$" **and** $1/8$" **Round Punch:** McGill, Inc.
Gold Pen: ZIG® Opaque Writer by EK Success Ltd.
Ring Die Cuts: Ellison® Craft & Design
Stickers: The Gifted Line®
Page Designer: Kim Skinner for Memory Lane

© & ™ Ellison® Craft & Design

The keepsake paper is reminiscent of the various milestones in a wonderful life and creates the perfect mood for this special photo. Mat the photo on yellow using scissors and punches, then mat again on tan and white. Journal on white and mat on tan, then arrange on keepsake paper.

Keepsake Patterned Paper: Frances Meyer Inc.®
Scissors: Seagull Paper Edgers by Fiskars®, Inc.
$1/4$" **Round Punch:** McGill, Inc.
Page Designer: LeNae Gerig for Hot Off The Press

Mom took this picture of me at the church ~ minutes before the big moment!

Overlap the photos with the laser lace paper to vary the look of your pages. Crop two photos into 5" tall ovals and one into a 6" tall oval. Double-mat each, then arrange on the yellow roses paper. Overlap to highlight the important areas, placing the 6" tall oval on the right as shown. Cut the laser lace into four pieces, mat and place one at each corner. Notice how the light yellow and white mats echo the lace at the corners and bring out the yellow in the bride's bouquet.

Yellow Roses Patterned Paper: *Paper Pizazz™ Romantic Papers* by Hot Off The Press
Laser Lace: *Paper Pizazz™ Romantic Papers* by Hot Off The Press
Scissors: Mini Victorian by Family Treasures
Page Designer: LeNae Gerig for Hot Off The Press

Formal wedding portraits can be used in conjunction with other pictures or keepsakes. This photo was triple-matted and placed on a page with the matted wedding invitation. Once the large rose embellishment is added, the page is a mini album of the wedding—showing the dress, colors, bouquet, invitation, bride and groom all on one page.

Green Marble Patterned Paper: *Paper Pizazz™ Very Pretty Papers* by Hot Off The Press
Rose Cutout: *Paper Pizazz™ Wedding* by Hot Off The Press
Scissors: Colonial Paper Edgers by Fiskars®, Inc.
Page Designer: LeNae Gerig for Hot Off The Press

Trim a piece of tan paper to 8"x10½" and glue to a burgundy handmade sheet. Glue a 7¼" wide strip of letters paper to the center of the tan page. Crop two photos into ovals. Mat an uncropped photo on letters paper. Mat again on black, then antique laces paper before placing in the center of the letters strip. Arrange the cropped photos on the top and bottom as shown, tucking one behind the center photo. Journal in the plain tan areas and draw a decorative border around two photos. Make one part of the journaling fun and one part informative.

Antique Laces Patterned Paper: *Paper Pizazz™ Pretty Papers* by Hot Off The Press
Burgundy Handmade Patterned Paper: *Paper Pizazz™ Handmade Papers* by Hot Off The Press
Letters Patterned Paper: *Paper Pizazz™ Black & White Photos* by Hot Off The Press
Page Designer: Allison Myers for Memory Lane

Occasionally it's nice to mat your photos in unusual ways, such as the "slip slots" on these photos and hearts. Use a ruler to make two 2" wide muted roses strips and glue them down each side of the page. Embellish the edges of the strips with a gold pen. Double mat each photo, keeping a plain mat on the outside to separate the photos from the background. Use a template to cut and mat two hearts. Cut ⅛" wide strips and glue to one shoulder of each heart and two corners of each photo. Journal with a black pen and create many dots around the heart edges and photo strips with a gold pen.

Muted Roses Patterned Paper: *Paper Pizazz™ Pretty Papers* by Hot Off The Press
Gold Pen: ZIG® Opaque Writer by EK Success Ltd.
Heart Template: Extra Special Products
Rulers: Déjà Views™ by C-Thru® Ruler Co.
Page Designer: LeNae Gerig for Hot Off The Press

Embossed frames can be used on a page as a single mat or in conjunction with other mats. This entire page serves as a mat for the photo and directs the eye downward and inward to the journaling.

Embossed Frame: Creative Card Company
Corner Cutter: Marvy® Uchida
Scissors: Mini Antique Elegance by Family Treasures
Stickers: The Gifted Line®
Page Designer: Ann Smith for Memory Lane

There is more to the wedding day than the bride's big moment. This lovely page features the bride's colors; however, it is obvious that Andrew was a big part of the wedding! The center is cut out of the lattice page and glued to the center of the yellow roses paper. The photos are matted on gold. The rose (pattern on page 142) is cut from light yellow and dark green and the two are combined as shown. The yellow is then matted on dark yellow. Add journaling to fill the empty areas.

Lattice Patterned Paper: *Paper Pizazz™ Wedding* by Hot Off The Press
Metallic Gold Paper: *Paper Pizazz™ Metallic Papers* by Hot Off The Press
Yellow Roses Patterned Paper: *Paper Pizazz™ Very Pretty Papers* by Hot Off The Press
Rose Die Cut: Ellison® Craft & Design
Page Designer: Becky Goughnour for Hot Off The Press

Accent your page with 3-D effects such as this sheer ribbon. This relatively simple page is given a touch of elegance by tying a shoestring bow with the ribbon and gluing it overlapping the journaling. The color picks up the subtle purple in the background paper and softens the blunt photo edges.

Patterned Paper: Frances Meyer Inc.®
1" wide Sheer Purple Ribbon: C.M. Offray & Son, Inc.
Page Designer: Sherri Johnston for Pebbles in My Pocket

© & ™ Ellison® Craft & Design

Not all wedding pages need to be formal! Embossed balloons add a festive touch to the already bright swirls. Bright mats and simple journaling accent the colorful party theme. Note that the page uses balloons in four colors, arranged in the corners to move the eye around the page.

Lavender Swirl Patterned Paper: *Paper Pizazz™ Very Pretty Papers* by Hot Off The Press
Balloon Die Cuts: Ellison® Craft & Design
Gold Pen: ZIG® Opaque Writer by EK Success Ltd.
Page Designer: Becky Goughnour for Hot Off The Press

™ Ellison® Craft & Design

Disney characters © Disney Enterprises, Inc.

The large, formal photo is placed at the top of the page and framed with gold scrolls, creating the focal point of the page. The smaller photos and journaling underneath expand on the day's activities, taking the viewer from the wedding to the fun of the reception.

Burgundy Handmade Patterned Paper: *Paper Pizazz™ Handmade Papers* by Hot Off The Press
Tapestry Patterned Paper: *Paper Pizazz™ Very Pretty Papers* by Hot Off The Press
Corner Cutter: Nostalgia Corner Edgers by Fiskars®, Inc.
Gold Pen: ZIG® Opaque Writer by EK Success Ltd.
Dark Gold Pen: Marvy® Uchida Gel Writer
Page Designer: LeNae Gerig for Hot Off The Press

This page makes good use of texture and contrast in its mats by using corner cutters on some mats as well as different colors, types of papers and mat widths. Insert the journaling over the mats, slightly into the photo to draw the eye from the regularity of the mats and add another level of interest.

Pressed Pansy and Purple Handmade Patterned Papers: *Paper Pizazz™ Handmade Papers* by Hot Off The Press
Corner Cutter: Nostalgia Corner Edgers by Fiskars®, Inc.
Silver Pen: Marvy® Uchida Gel Roller
Page Designer: LeNae Gerig for Hot Off The Press

Creating a wedding album

These pages demonstrate how to create a wedding album using the bride's colors and a variety of photos from the different wedding stages—engagement, shower, wedding, reception and honeymoon. These pages were created by Wendy's mother, Becky Goughnour, and bridesmaid, LeNae Gerig, using her colors: forest green, white and a touch of pink.

The wedding album should start with the beginning of the process—the engagement announcement. Use a non-wedding related photo and color photocopy newspaper articles onto acid-free paper. Treat the articles as photos, matting and cropping as normal; however, be sure to keep surrounding historical information. Arrange on a sheet of green swirl paper, trim as shown then mat on dark green before gluing to the gold sheet. Add a matted heart embellishment between the items to connect the elements and soften the edges.

Green Swirl Patterned Paper: *Paper Pizazz™ Pretty Papers* by Hot Off The Press
Metallic Gold Paper: *Paper Pizazz™ Metallic Papers* by Hot Off The Press
Heart Charm Cutouts: *Paper Pizazz™ Embellishments* by Hot Off The Press
Scissors: Mini Antique by Family Treasures
Page Designer: Becky Goughnour for Hot Off The Press

This casual yet feminine page is created by silhouetting two photos of Wendy and contrasting them to a shot of her and her grandmothers. The effect highlights Wendy and allows a fun look while still showing the sentimentality and closeness of the occasion. Notice the silhouetted photo is placed on a round mat. Decorative scissors and punches embellish the edges of the page and journaling.

Cream Roses Patterned Paper: *Paper Pizazz™ Pretty Papers* by Hot Off The Press
Metallic Gold Paper: *Paper Pizazz™ Metallic Papers* by Hot Off The Press
Scissors: Cloud and Seagull Paper Edgers by Fiskars®, Inc.
⅛" Round Punch: McGill, Inc.
Green Pen: ZIG® Writer by EK Success Ltd.
Page Designer: Becky Goughnour for Hot Off The Press

This page is made easy by taking advantage of coordinating papers. Trim a piece of tri-dots on pink paper to 7"x9½", mat on burgundy then glue to the center of the tri-dot on light green paper. Crop the photos and mat on combinations of light green, dark green, burgundy and white. Journaling on the mats provides a personal touch to each photo.

Tri Dots on Pink and Tri-Dots on Light Green Patterned Papers: *Paper Pizazz™ Light Great Backgrounds* by Hot Off The Press

Scissors: Ripple Paper Edgers by Fiskars®, Inc.

Page Designer: Becky Goughnour for Hot Off The Press

Don't forget the groom in your wedding album! The same colors that have made feminine pages can be used to make masculine pages. Strong forest green and white stripes along with green, silver and black mats complement the black and white tuxedos of the groom, best man and attendants. The corners were created with a corner cutter, adding an elegant and old-fashioned touch to an otherwise stark page.

Green & White Striped Patterned Paper: Paper Patch®

Metallic Silver Paper: Hygloss Products, Inc.

Corner Cutter: Regal Corner Edgers by Fiskars®, Inc.

Silver Pen: Marvy® Uchida Gel Roller

Page Designer: LeNae Gerig for Hot Off The Press

Getting ready deserves a special page; after all, dressing-up is part of the wedding fun! Notice that the two pages are not alike in layout, yet there can be little doubt they go together. The same papers, scissors, punches and photo shapes link the pages. The first page features Wendy and is elaborately journaled while the second shows other moments of the fun.

Watercolor Roses Patterned Paper: *Paper Pizazz™ Romantic Papers* by Hot Off The Press

Scissors: Cloud and Scallop Paper Edgers by Fiskars®, Inc.

Green Calligraphy Pen: ZIG® Calligraphy by EK Success Ltd.

Green and Pink Pen: ZIG® Writer by EK Success Ltd.

White Pen: ZIG® Opaque Writer by EK Success Ltd.

Fleur De Lis Punch: Family Treasures

Page Designer: Becky Goughnour for Hot Off The Press

This Moment from *Paper Pizazz™ Inspirations & Celebrations*

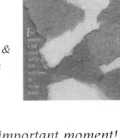

Finally the ceremony, the most important moment! Muted tones with an inspirational inscription offer the perfect page for these touching photos. Take extra time with the journaling and mats, embellishing the edges and creating flourishes—but leave the photos uncropped so the viewer can see everything.

Pink Handmade Patterned Paper: *Paper Pizazz™ Handmade Papers* by Hot Off The Press

This Moment Patterned Paper: *Paper Pizazz™ Inspirations & Celebrations* by Hot Off The Press

Scissors: Deckle Paper Edgers by Fiskars®, Inc.

Thick Gold Pen: ZIG® Opaque Writer by EK Success Ltd.

Thin Gold Pen: Marvy® Uchida Gel Roller

Page Designer: Becky Goughnour for Hot Off The Press

The wedding portrait should be treated differently than other wedding photos. It should show the care and details that went into the wedding. Here is where the bride's colors should really come into play. Wendy's colors, which have been used throughout this album, are used exclusively on this page. This page's three dimensional appearance is created by carefully cutting around the ribbons in the patterned paper with a craft knife. Slip the matted corners underneath the ribbons.

Ribbons & Charms Patterned Paper: *Paper Pizazz™ Wedding* by Hot Off The Press
Scissors: Colonial Paper Edgers by Fiskars®, Inc.
Craft Knife: X-acto® by Hunt
Page Designer: LeNae Gerig for Hot Off The Press

Ribbons & Charms from *Paper Pizazz™ Wedding*

The honeymoon photos provide a perfect ending for your wedding album. Have some fun with the colors, but stick to the same basic color scheme. Also, differentiate the honeymoon from the rest of the pages. A casual background paper and fun matting do an excellent job of distinguishing this page from the formality of the rest of the album.

Oatmeal Handmade Patterned Paper: *Paper Pizazz™ Solid Muted Tones* by Hot Off The Press
Sand & Shells Patterned Paper: Paper Patch®
Scissors: Ripple Paper Edgers by Fiskars®, Inc.
Page Designer: Becky Goughnour for Hot Off The Press

Christmas

The holiday season always brings cheer, food, family and tons of photos! You may want to create an album that's exclusively Christmas photos. This chapter shows you techniques that can make each year's photos exceptional, including a few not shown in other chapters! For example, there are many ways to use rubber stamps to create a different look. The albums shown on pages 86–87 use four stamping techniques to decorate your Christmas photos.

At the bottom of page 88, an album page is designed like a Christmas card. The traditional solid red and plaid papers create a homey feel as warm as the background in the photo. The lively feel of the polka dot background echoes the action of gift opening in the two-page spread at the bottom of page 89. We really liked the symbolism used at the bottom of page 93, where the photo mats are "tied" with "ribbon" and stacked like so many presents under the tree.

Of course, real ribbon can be used. This is done at the top of page 93; the ribbon holly flowers add texture to the page, while the adhesive ribbon corners provide a great "border." Adhesive ribbon is the newest addition to the growing list of memory album products, and we have come across some really excellent ideas for working it into your page designs.

The hustle and bustle of the Christmas season is done. Now you can warm yourself with the rewards of your work as you re-live the day making all those photos into beautiful album pages!

The border for this section was created using a ruler template from Deja Views™ by C-Thru® Ruler Co.

Rubber stamping can be an excellent memory album tool. Glue the photos inside the frames. Stamp two extra checked frames of each color on a separate piece of paper and cut them apart to make the borders. The remaining stamps are stamped with black ink and sprinkled with clear embossing powder which is melted with a heat gun, then colored with markers.

Clear Embossing Powder: Rubber Stampede®
Ink Pads: Rubber Stampede®
Pigment Ink Markers: Rubber Stampede®
Rubber Stamps: Rubber Stampede®
Page Designer: Lynn Damelio for Rubber Stampede®

Use embossing ink to stamp several pine sprigs onto dark green paper. Before the ink dries, sprinkle gold embossing powder over the images. Tap the excess powder back into the bottle. Use a heat gun to melt the powder. Stamp and emboss the frames onto tan paper with the same technique. The poinsettias and banner are stamped with red ink, then covered with clear embossing powder. Cut them out and arrange on the page with the photos.

Embossing Ink Pad: Rubber Stampede®
Gold Embossing Powder: Rubber Stampede®
Red Ink Pad: Rubber Stampede®
Rubber Stamps: Rubber Stampede®
Page Designer: Grace Taormina for Rubber Stampede®

Use the pattern to draw and cut out ¼" wide white strips; glue them to border the page. For variety, mat some photos and silhouette another. Stamp several gingerbread men of different sizes with black ink and sprinkle with clear embossing powder. Use a heat gun to melt the powder, then use markers to color the gingerbread men. Cut out and glue to the page, filling the empty areas.

Black Ink Pad: Rubber Stampede®
Clear Embossing Powder: Rubber Stampede®
Pigment Ink Markers: Rubber Stampede®
Rubber Stamps: Rubber Stampede®
Scissors: Scallop Paper Edgers by Fiskars®, Inc.
Page Designer: Lynn Damelio for Rubber Stampede®

Use different ink pad colors to create a border around a page. Working on one section at a time, stamp dark green boughs first, leaving spaces between them, then stamp light green boughs in the empty spaces. Sprinkle clear embossing powder over the stamps and heat to melt. Use different markers to color directly on the bell stamp, stamping a variety of colored bells (clean the stamp between colors). Emboss using the same technique, then arrange with the matted photos on the page. Stamp and emboss a banner. Journal in your own handwriting.

Ink Pads: Rubber Stampede®
Matte Sticker Paper: Rubber Stampede®
Blue Pen: ZIG® Writer by EK Success Ltd.
Purple, Red and Yellow Watercolor Markers: Rubber Stampede®
Rubber Stamps: Rubber Stampede®
Page Designer: Lynn Damelio for Rubber Stampede®

One photo "falling" off the page keeps this page fun and balances the page elements. The candy die cuts work as connectors, guiding the eye from the photos to the journaling and back again.

Pine Trees Patterned Paper: *Paper Pizazz™ Vacation* by Hot Off The Press
Candy Die Cuts: Pebbles in My Pocket
Page Designer: Launa Naylor for Pebbles in My Pocket

A page like this one could be color photocopied and used as a cover page for the annual Christmas newsletter! This informal portrait is matted four times, then glued to the center of a trimmed red sheet matted on polka dot paper. Corners are added to the page and empty spaces are filled with journaling stickers. What an impression your Christmas letter will make!

Plaid Pine Trees, Poinsettia Check and White Polka Dot Patterned Papers: Paper Patch®
Alphabet Stickers: Making Memories™
Holly Stickers: ©Mrs. Grossman's Paper Co.
Page Designer: Dawn Chapman for Memory Lane

Use a circle template to cut six ornaments, then use punches to create a decorative band along the center of each. Glue colored paper behind each ornament to show through the punches. Use a square punch to make the ornament tops, trimming the lower edge with decorative scissors. Glue the ornaments to the page top, using a gold pen to "hang" them. Double-mat a photo and glue the remaining ornaments beside it. Use stickers to journal the date.

Metallic Gold and Silver Papers: Hygloss Products, Inc.
Pine Boughs and Red & Green Stripe Patterned Papers: *Paper Pizazz™ Christmas* by Hot Off The Press
Scissors: Scallop Paper Edgers by Fiskars®, Inc.
$\frac{1}{16}$", $\frac{1}{8}$" and $\frac{1}{4}$" Round Punches: McGill, Inc.
Corner Cutter: McGill, Inc.
Gold Pen: ZIG Opaque Writer by E.K. Success Ltd.
Number Stickers: Making Memories™
Star, Gingerbread Man, Diamond, Note, Square, Rectangle and Heart Punches: McGill, Inc.
Page Designer: Debbie Hewitt

These facing pages are laid out as mirror images. Trim two 2" wide green strips with patterned scissors and glue to the outer edges of the dotted sheets. Place stickers were placed on the green strips. Double-mat the photos and journaling on plain and patterned paper.

Ho Ho Ho and White Dots on Red Patterned Papers: *Paper Pizazz™ Ho Ho Ho!!!* by Hot Off The Press
Red and Green Pens: ZIG® Millennium by EK Success Ltd.
Scissors: Victorian Paper Edgers by Fiskars®, Inc.
Design Line: ©Mrs. Grossman's Paper Co.
Alphabet and Bell Stickers: ©Mrs. Grossman's Paper Co.
Page Designer: Debbie Peterson

When you have an empty area on your page, die cuts are a quick and easy way to fill it. Use a corrugator for the candle to add texture to the page. Mat the photos on solid papers to pick up the colors in the plaid paper.

Metallic Gold Paper: *Paper Pizazz™ Metallic Papers* by Hot Off The Press

Red Tartan Patterned Paper: *Paper Pizazz™ Christmas* by Hot Off The Press

Scissors: Colonial and Majestic Paper Edgers by Fiskars®, Inc.

¹/₄" Round Punch: McGill, Inc.

Candle and Holly Die Cuts: Pebbles in My Pocket

Corrugator: Gil Mechanical Tube Wringer

Page Designer: Nancy Church for Pebbles in My Pocket

Attach the ribbon to red paper and trim ¹/₄" larger on each side. Glue the matted ribbon around the page to create a frame. Attach a ribbon poinsettia to each corner. Use a template to crop and mat the photos into hearts. Cut out three extra hearts and arrange the elements as shown. Use stickers and ribbon ornaments to embellish the page. Journal on the extra hearts and inside the mats.

³/₄" wide Red/Green Plaid Ribbon: Self-Adhesive Memory Book Ribbon by C.M. Offray & Son, Inc.

1³/₄" wide Ribbon Poinsettias: C.M. Offray & Son, Inc.

Holly Stickers: ©Mrs. Grossman's Paper Co.

Scissors: Deckle Paper Edgers by Fiskars®, Inc.

Template: Extra Special Products

Page Designer: Carla Spence for C.M. Offray & Son, Inc.

These two mats use the same colors, but vary in width to create an interesting arrangement. The die cut at the top of the photo frames the picture and moves the eye to the rest of page.

Ho Ho Ho Patterned Paper: *Paper Pizazz™ Ho Ho Ho!!!* by Hot Off The Press
Holly Die Cut: Ellison® Craft & Design
Computer Typeface: D.J. Inkers™
Page Designer: Launa Naylor for Pebbles in My Pocket

Consider the dimensions of the headline before beginning; choose lettering big enough to fill the page but not so big that the words run off the page. Trace and mat the lettering as for the photos. Leave an extra inch below the photos to allow space for journaling or decorating. The gingerbread die cuts connect with the photos' theme, while the heart berries echo the heart buttons on the gingerbread people.

Christmas Plaid Patterned Paper: *Paper Pizazz™ Christmas* by Hot Off The Press
Gingerbread Die Cuts: Pebbles in My Pocket
Heart and Holly Punches: Family Treasures
Lettering Template: Pebbles in My Pocket
Page Designer: Erika Clayton for Pebbles in My Pocket

Though Christmas pages tend to have a certain color scheme, there is no reason other colors can't work. This page's winter tones pick up the colors in Chad's costume. Use a corner template to cut the corners, mat and place in each corner. Crop and mat the photos, then use the ruler to draw the staff lines. Add a treble cleft and several notes to the staff before journaling. Use the pattern to create the trees. Follow the manufacturer's instructions to apply liquid applique for snow.

Corner Template: Keeping Memories Alive™
Liquid Applique: Marvy® Uchida
Scissors: Deckle Papers Edgers by Fiskars®, Inc.
Ruler Template: Déjà Views™ by C-Thru® Ruler Co.
Page Designer: Debbie Peterson

Use your photos to "build" a house. Cut the roof top (pattern on page 142) with straight edges scissors and the underside with decorative scissors to mimic snow. Cut a 1½" wide foundation and a ½" wide corner in the same manner. Glue the pieces over two photos, then embellish the scene with a chimney and Punch-Outs™. Crop and mat another photo into a smoke shape and glue above the chimney. Use a 1" strip for the snowy ground. Journal on the Punch-Outs™.

Snowflakes Patterned Paper: *Paper Pizazz™ Christmas* by Hot Off The Press
Snowflakes Punch-Outs™: *Paper Pizazz™ Holidays & Seasons Punch-Outs™* by Hot Off The Press
Scissors: Cloud Papers Edgers by Fiskars®, Inc.
Calligraphy Pen: ZIG® Calligraphy by EK Success Ltd.
Page Designer: Marci Kearns

Attach ribbon to green paper and trim ¹/₄" larger on each side. Glue three matted ribbons to opposite corners as shown. Crop two photos into ovals and mat them on rectangles. Double-mat two uncropped photos. Arrange the matted photos on the page. Add ribbon poinsettias to the corners of two photos. Glue the ribbon wreath below another photo to balance the page. Use stickers to journal in the empty area.

⁵/₈" wide Ribbon: Self-Adhesive Memory Book Ribbon by C.M. Offray & Son, Inc.

1³/₄" wide Ribbon Poinsettias and 2" wide Wreath: C.M. Offray & Son, Inc.

Scissors: Heartbeat Paper Edgers by Fiskars®, Inc.

Stickers: ©Mrs. Grossman's Paper Co.

Page Designer: Carla Spence for C.M. Offray & Son, Inc.

Sometimes a die cut can inspire a page idea. Make this package scene by using die cut bows and tags with square matted photos. Vary the package sizes to add interest and fun. Tie two packages by adding a ¹/₂" wide strip to one corner. Thin white mats help separate the photos from the printed mats.

Red/White Gingham, Red/White Polka Dot, Red/White Stripe, Green/White Check, Green/White Gingham Patterned Papers: Paper Patch®

Bow and Tag Die Cuts: Ellison® Craft & Design

Page Designer: Launa Naylor for Pebbles in My Pocket

© & ™ Ellison® Craft & Design

© & ™ Ellison® Craft & Design

93

Special Days

Often, it's special days such as birthdays, Easter, Halloween, New Year's, Valentine's Day, Thanksgiving or Hanukkah that produce so many photographs. And if it's symbolic to your family, it's worthy of superior treatment! This chapter features plenty of ideas to create an album page as special as the day. From enhancing a single photograph at the bottom of page 98, to a spread of eight photographs at the bottom of page 100, this section provides lots of techniques to use.

Die cuts can easily set different moods, such as at the top of page 97 where the die cut flower pot is used to hold die cut flowers and a silhouette cut "Easter bunny." Yet at the bottom of page 101, a few color coordinated die cut leaves provide a tender touch to this masculine Thanksgiving page. At the tops of pages 100 and 101, die cuts were used to create an entire scene to place your photographs into. But don't mistake that clever scene at the top of page 99 for a die cut—that's a patterned paper! The "windows" are cut out to frame strategically placed photos. You can see the un-cut version of the paper in the inset to the right.

A unique twist to memory album pages is the "interactive" page. It combines the traditional concept of inclusion of memorabilia with the new idea of photo embellishment. This section includes three such pages. At the bottom of page 102 a "pocket" is made to hold wrapping paper from a special present. At the top of the same page, a die cut pattern was used to make a pop-up card! Page 105 also uses a die cut pattern to make a pull-out section that displays tiny silhouette cut photos! The possibilities are endless, as you are discovering!

The border for this section was created using Aztec Paper Edgers by Fiskars®, Inc.

New Year: Take inspiration from the clothes and start with paisley patterned and plain bright papers to create the backgrounds. Trim the mat paper to the same size and shape of the photo. Then offset the mat ¹/₂". One large star provides journaling while punched stars fill the empty areas.

Blue Paisley Patterned
Paper: *Paper Pizazz™ 1950's & '60's* by Hot Off The Press
Star Punch: Marvy® Uchida
Star Template: Extra Special Products
Page Designer: Katie Hacker for Hot Off The Press

Valentine: Duplicate the colors in the photo with the papers you select. Red, white and black papers create a stunning, coordinated effect. Trim a piece of white paper to 7"x10" and glue to the center of a patterned piece. Cut the heart from patterned paper and mat using patterned scissors. Double-mat two other photos and arrange as shown. Punch several small patterned and plain hearts and arrange near the photos in the empty areas. Use a black pen to journal and draw other embellishments.

Red/White Check, Plaid and Gingham
Patterned Papers: Paper Patch®
Scissors: Jumbo Lace Scallop by Family Treasures
Heart Punch: Marvy® Uchida
Heart Template: Extra Special Products
Page Designer: Allison Myers for Memory Lane

Easter:

Create a small bouquet with a die cut vase and flowers. Tuck a silhouetted photo inside the vase to add a unique touch for the careful viewer. The heart and ½" rose paper squares placed ½" apart bring fun to the page and fill up empty spaces. For extra depth, place photo on foam dots to raise it above the other page elements.

Muted Roses Patterned Paper: *Paper Pizazz*™ *Wedding* by Hot Off The Press
Flower and Basket Die Cuts: Ellison® Craft & Design
Self-adhesive Foam Dots: All Night Media®, Inc.
Stickers: ©Mrs. Grossman's Paper Co.
White Pen: ZIG® Writer by EK Success Ltd.
Page Designer: Sandi Genovese for Ellison® Craft & Design

Easter 1997

Create your own colorful background by layering colored and white strips. Cut an 8"x10½" piece of tan paper. Cut 1"x10¼" strips of pink, yellow, blue, green and purple paper and glue across the tan paper. Place 1" wide white strips over the colored strips, leaving a ⅛" space between to let the colors show through. Mat the photos and journal on similar colors. Add stickers at the top and bottom of the page. Hang the egg stickers with a yellow pen. Mat the tan on a full sheet of dark brown paper.

Yellow with White Dots Patterned Paper: Paper Patch®
Stickers: ©Mrs. Grossman's Paper Co.
Yellow Pen: ZIG® Writer by EK Success Ltd.
Page Designer: Ann Smith for Memory Lane

Easter

Garrett hunting eggs at Grandma's March 1997

© Expressly Portraits

Glue two sheets of pink moiré paper together into a 10"x11" sheet. Glue to the center of a 12"x12" white sheet. Place the egg border stickers around the edges of the paper. Trim the corners of a 7½"x9¾" portrait and add a pink moiré scrap under each. Mat the photo on a full sheet of pastel quilt paper. Glue the matted photo angled to the page. Place the large stickers at the bottom and on the corners as shown.

Pastel Quilt Patterned Paper:
  Paper Pizazz™ Baby by Hot Off The Press
Pink Moiré Patterned Paper:
  Paper Pizazz™ Wedding by Hot Off The Press
Corner Cutter: Art Deco Corner Edgers by Fiskars®, Inc.
Stickers: The Gifted Line®
Page Designer: Stephanie Taylor

Halloween:

Have your album page tell a fictional story! Use a color copier to enlarge a photo, silhouette it and mat on tan paper. Trim purple paper and place on a sheet of orange. Mat a black skyline die cut (pattern on page 141) on tan and glue to the bottom of the page. Use a silver pen to draw more windows in the die cut. Place candy stickers on the thought balloon. Glue the thought balloon and the photo to the page, journaling in the empty areas.

Skyline Die Cut: Ellison® Craft & Design
Silver Pen: ZIG® Opaque Writer by EK Success Ltd.
Stickers: ©Mrs. Grossman's Paper Co.
Page Designer: Carrie DuWelius for Memory Lane

Pages such as this are a spectacular addition to any memory album, yet they take only minutes and provide a space for many small snapshots. Choose a pre-designed page and simply cut out the windows, insert a photo or journaling.

Haunted House Patterned Paper: *Paper Pizazz™ Holidays & Seasons* by Hot Off The Press
Craft Knife: X-acto® by Hunt
Page Designer: Katie Hacker for Hot Off The Press

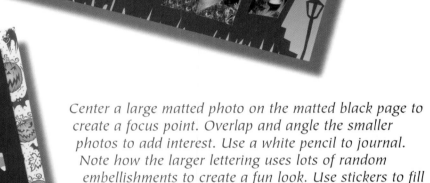

Haunted House from *Paper Pizazz™ Holidays & Seasons*

Center a large matted photo on the matted black page to create a focus point. Overlap and angle the smaller photos to add interest. Use a white pencil to journal. Note how the larger lettering uses lots of random embellishments to create a fun look. Use stickers to fill the empty areas.

Bat & Pumpkin and Black & White Check Patterned Papers: Paper Patch®
Lettering Template: Pebbles Funky ABC Tracer by Pebbles in My Pocket
Stickers: ©Mrs. Grossman's Paper Co.
White Colored Pencil: EK Success Ltd.
Page Designer: Ann Smith for Memory Lane

Mix print and solid papers for a great look! Use a template to make the stars, moon and pumpkins. Assemble these and several die cuts into a scene. Use a black pen to add stitches or other details on the elements. Trim the photos to fit inside the largest shapes. Journal and add a few pumpkin tendrils with a silver pen.

Orange & White Print, Green & White Print, Black & White Check and Wood Patterned Papers: Northern Spy
Fence and Leaf Die Cuts: Accu/Cut® Systems
Moon, Pumpkin and Star Templates: Provo Craft®
Silver Pen: Marvy® Uchida Gel Roller
Page Designer: Allison Myers for Memory Lane

Experiment with free form shapes that match your theme—a stem added to a simple oval or circle makes an instant pumpkin. Create a carefree feeling by placing the photos at various angles. The woven bands are a great final touch, connecting the two pages and providing a perfect space for journaling. Cut a 1 1/4" strip then slice 3/4" wide bands 1 1/4" apart. Weave a 1/2" wide strip through the slices. Mat on yellow then use a template to create the journaling ovals. Use the pattern to make the swirls.

Autumn Leaves Patterned Paper: *Paper Pizazz™ Holidays & Seasons* by Hot Off The Press
Scissors: Dragon-Back and Volcano Paper Edgers by Fiskars®, Inc.
Craft Knife: X-acto® by Hunt
Pen: ZIG® Writer by EK Success Ltd.
Page Designer: Katie Hacker for Hot Off The Press

Fence die cuts are a great way to start scenic pages. Trim dark blue paper and use a punch to create many stars. Place yellow paper under the punched stars. Double-mat the punched paper with a bright orange plain paper and a light orange print paper. Mat the photo on orange and a house die cut on purple. Use a template to make the moon; use a punch for the pumpkin and ghost. Layer and glue the elements to the page as shown.

Orange & White Polka Dot Patterned Paper: Paper Patch®
Scissors: Pinking Paper Edgers by Fiskars®, Inc.
Fence Die Cut: Accu/Cut® Systems
Ghost, Pumpkin and Star Punches: McGill, Inc.
House Die Cut: Pebbles in My Pocket
Witch Die Cut: Ellison® Craft & Design
Page Designer: Kim Skinner for Memory Lane

© & ™ Ellison® Craft & Design

Thanksgiving: Create a quick and easy page by selecting a patterned paper and using coordinating colors for the matting and die cuts. The color scheme of this page creates a subtly masculine as well as fall-toned page. The leaves in the lower left corner balance the journaling square.

Brown Plaid Patterned Paper: *Paper Pizazz™ Great Outdoors* by Hot Off The Press
Scissors: Deckle Paper Edgers by Fiskars®, Inc.
Scissors: Jumbo Deckle by Family Treasures
Leaf Die Cuts: Little Red Wagon
Photo Corners: Canson®
Page Designer: Allison Myers for Memory Lane

Hanukkah: *This simple page pops-up! Use stickers to make the outer frame. Journal on the banner and add stickers. Fold a 11½"x6" piece of white paper in half. Glue the center of the die cut pop-up into it. Glue a 5"x5¼" blue rectangle to the front of the folded white paper. Glue to the center of the framed page. Insert into a page protector and gently cut the sheet protector around three sides of the pop-up. Decorate the front with a die cut and silhouetted photo and add a silhouetted photo to the inside pop-up, as well as a border and menorah. (Star of David pattern on page 140. Banner pattern on page 141.)*

Polka Dot Patterned Paper: Paper Patch®
Banner, Pop-Up and Star Die Cuts: Ellison® Craft & Design
Blue Pen: Marvy® Uchida
Design Line and Stickers: ©Mrs. Grossman's Paper Co.
Page Designer: Sandi Genovese for Ellison® Craft & Design

Birthdays:

This pocket page is meant to hold mementos! Use double-sided tape around three edges of a 7¼"x6" black paper to make the pocket. Insert the memento wrapping paper into the pocket. Cut the mask, glue to the pocket and punch a hole in one side. Insert the ends of five 12" lengths of ribbon into the hole and knot the ends. Glue the die cuts as shown, adding journaling in the empty areas. (Mask pattern on page 138. Noisemaker patterns on page 140.)

Black and White Check Patterned Paper: Paper Patch®
¼" **Round Punch:** McGill, Inc.
¼" **wide Satin Ribbon:** C.M. Offray & Son, Inc.
Alphabet Stickers: LetterEase by Ellison® Craft & Design
Balloon, Favor and Mask Die Cuts: Ellison® Craft & Design
Design Line and Stickers: ©Mrs. Grossman's Paper Co.
Page Designer: Sandi Genovese for Ellison® Craft & Design

Try to create a different look for each birthday. This simple page conveys both the fun and humor of a 40th birthday. Double-mat a group photo and silhouette another. Glue to the page as shown. Use a computer to journal the "story," cut out and mat. Use stickers to decorate the top of the page, adding a headline when finished.

Black & White Gingham and Dots Patterned Papers: Paper Patch®
Metallic Gold Paper: *Paper Pizazz™ Metallic Papers* by Hot Off The Press
Alphabet and Confetti Stickers: ©Mrs. Grossman's Paper Co.
Page Designer: Kim McCrary for Pebbles in My Pocket

One of the most effective ways to link two pages is to extend a headline across them. Press the alphabet stickers to white paper, cut out and double-mat. Use similar papers and punches on both pages. Varying the angles of the photos and breaking the page border adds a playful touch. (Star patterns on pages 122–123.)

Balloon and Navy & White Polka Dot Patterned Papers: Paper Patch®
Alphabet Stickers: Frances Meyer Inc.®
Star Die Cuts: Ellison® Craft & Design
Star Punches: Family Treasures
Page Designer: Ann Smith for Memory Lane

This headline neatly guides the eye to the next page. The triangular photo arrangements provide easy but interesting designs. Die cut balloons are used to fill empty areas as well as balance the page. Each photo is double-matted with a ¹/₂" margin on the bottom for journaling. (Balloon patterns on page 78.)

Confetti Patterned Paper:
  Paper Pizazz™ Birthday by Hot Off The Press
Balloon and Number Die Cuts: Ellison® Craft & Design
Lettering Template: Pebbles in My Pocket
Page Designer: Launa Naylor for Pebbles in My Pocket

© & ™ Accu/Cut® Systems

Punches, die cuts and patterned strips can be combined to make new objects like the ornaments on this birthday cake. Cut two ¹/₂" wide strips and glue to the cake. Punch a ¹/₁₆" hole in a ¹/₄" punch and glue to a second ¹/₄" circle so the color shows through. Glue these "flowers" to the frosting strips. Make "leaves" with a teardrop punch and glue near the flowers. The candle is corrugated and glued over the cake. Finally, glue a plate over the lower edge of the cake. Double-mat three photos and glue them, the cake and a matted journaling square to the page. Add some "flowers" with "leaves" in the empty areas.

Pink & White Gingham and Polka Dot Patterned Papers: Paper Patch®
Scissors: Seagull Paper Edgers by Fiskars®, Inc.
¹/₁₆" and ¹/₄" Round Punches: McGill, Inc.
Cake Die Cut: Accu/Cut® Systems
Computer Typeface: D.J. Inkers™
Corrugator: Paper Crimper by Fiskars®, Inc.
Teardrop Punch: McGill, Inc.
Page Designer: Kim McCrary for Pebbles in My Pocket

Creative matting can be the focus of the whole page! Use the pattern (see page 139) to make the hat brims. Trim the photos in a triangle shape and glue the pom-pom to the top. Trim a patterned sheet to 8"x10¹/₂", cut the corners and center on a plain sheet. Arrange the mats as shown, then arrange the journaling above and below. Add star punches to the hat brims to finish.

Confetti Patterned Paper: *Paper Pizazz™ Birthday* by Hot Off The Press
Scissors: Seagull Paper Edgers by Fiskars®, Inc.
Alphabet Stickers: Frances Meyer Inc.®
Star Punch: Family Treasures
Page Designer: Debbie Hewitt

See page 132 for tips on how to create this interactive, pull-out page. Use foam dots on the silhouette cut photo and the party favor bursts to add depth. Stickers, punches and die cuts enhance the page's theme, though there is no journaling. Pictures really do say a thousand words. (Noisemaker patterns on page 138. Balloon patterns on page 78.)

Red & White Check Patterned Paper: Paper Patch®
Red & White Stripes and White Dot on Red Patterned Papers: *Paper Pizazz™ Ho Ho Ho!!!* by Hot Off The Press
Balloon, Favor and Letter Die Cuts: Ellison® Craft & Design
Design Line and Stickers: ©Mrs. Grossman's Paper Co.
Heart Punch: Marvy® Uchida
Self-adhesive Foam Dots: All Night Media®, Inc.
Page Designer: Sandi Genovese for Ellison® Craft & Design

PAPER PIZAZZ™
OUR VACATIONS
18 ACID-FREE SHEETS FOR MEMORY ALBUMS, STAMPING & MORE!

LONDON

BEACH BABE

106

Vacation

Vacation photos offer us a chance to go a little wild with memory album products and techniques. Anything goes for these photos and this chapter illustrates plenty of ideas! The bottom of page 116 shows some amazing techniques for photo cropping. The tops of the mountains have been silhouette cut, then arranged to produce a mountain range across the top of the page and a waterfall effect down the center of the page. The result is nearly an optical illusion!

Look closely at the embellishing technique used at the top of page 113. The shells lying atop the photo edges aren't stickers—they are part of the background paper! A craft knife was used to carefully outline the shells, then the matted photos were slipped underneath them.

There are three collages in this section that go nuts combining photos, stickers, punches and die cuts to produce truly inspiring effects! At the bottom of page 111, the background paper produces the collage effect. At the bottom of page 112, it's the elements on the page that create the collage—then the photo is separated to stand on its own. At the top of page 117, stickers make a collage in the border. All methods are equally distinctive.

A very striking page is created with a technique called "splitting the page." It's exhibited at the top of page 110. The result is one of unity found through separation—an oxymoron only plausible in this zany chapter. No matter what your pleasure, you'll find that making memory pages of your vacation photographs will be as memorable as the trip itself!

The border for this section was created using
Deckle Paper Edgers by Fiskars®, Inc.

Begin this page by trimming two sides of a patterned paper and gluing it to a plain sheet. Crop two photos into 4½" tall ovals. Crop three action shots into 3¼" wide ovals. Arrange the large photos above the smaller photos, leaving the top right corner available for journaling. The cutouts give a finishing touch, allowing the viewer to understand the theme of the page at a glance.

Paddling Patterned Paper: *Paper Pizazz™ Great Outdoors* by Hot Off The Press
Fish and Pole Cutouts: *Paper Pizazz™ Masculine Papers* by Hot Off The Press
Scissors: Deckle and Mini Pinking Paper Edgers by Fiskars®, Inc.
Page Designer: Debbie Peterson

Though consistency can be nice, cropping and matting your photos in a variety of styles works too. The blue paper was embellished with penned snowflakes and dots and used for matting and the headline letters. Snowflake die cuts connect the photos and guide the eye from one area of the page to another.

Snowy Patterned Paper: MPR Paperbiliites™ III
Corner Cutter: Clover Lace by McGill, Inc.
Letters and Snow Die Cuts: Ellison® Craft & Design
White Pen: Marvy® Uchida Gel Roller
Page Designer: LeNae Gerig for Hot Off The Press

© & ™ Ellison® Craft & Design

Vacations produce many snapshots, and sometimes it's difficult to find a way to use them all. This page takes advantage of large die cuts to frame smaller photos. Use the wave die cuts to create the breakers at the bottom of the page. Arrange the sunglasses and sunburst above the breakers and mount them on cloud paper. Glue the sunglasses and sunbursts in place with the photos inside. Embellish the waves with a white pen. Add water drop stickers above the waves to create splashes and fill empty areas. Offset mat several photos and glue above the breakers. (The sunglasses pattern is on page 138.)

Clouds Patterned Paper: *Paper Pizazz™ Our Vacation* by Hot Off The Press

Splash Stickers: ©Mrs. Grossman's Paper Co.

Sunburst, Sunglasses and Waves Die Cuts: Ellison® Craft & Design

White Pen: Marvy® Uchida Gel Roller

Page Designer: Stephanie Taylor

© & ™ Ellison® Craft & Design

Creating an interesting page can take minutes with the right tools. Mat a photo on white, then use a corner cutter to trim. Mat on blue paper and glue to the page as shown. Mount the Punch-Outs™ on foam mounting tape and place on opposite sides of the photos. Run journaling along the opposite sides to balance the page.

Shells Patterned Paper: *Paper Pizazz™ Vacation* by Hot Off The Press

Sunglasses and Tree Punch-Outs™: *Paper Pizazz™ Vacation Punch-Outs™* by Hot Off The Press

Alphabet Stickers: Frances Meyer Inc.®

Corner Cutter: Regal Corner Edgers by Fiskars®, Inc.

Page Designer: Debbie Peterson

© & ™ Ellison® Craft & Design

Splitting a page is a great look for many pages. Trim a piece of blue chalk paper to 7³/₄"x8³/₄". Use a ruler with an elegant wave pattern to divide the trimmed piece into three asymmetrical pieces. Mat each piece and glue to the page, leaving ¹/₂" between each section. Cut letters out of contrasting paper, outline with a pen and glue to the page top. Mat two photos and silhouette a third photo. Glue to the page as shown, journaling in the open areas.

Blue Chalk Patterned Paper: *Paper Pizazz™ Light Great Backgrounds* by Hot Off The Press
Raindrops Patterned Paper: *Paper Pizazz™ Child's Play* by Hot Off The Press
Ruler: Déjà Views™ by C-Thru® Ruler Co.
Page Designer: Becky Goughnour for Hot Off The Press

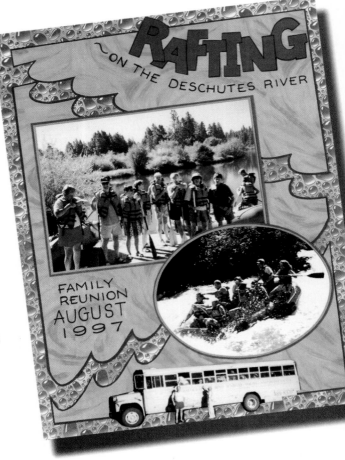

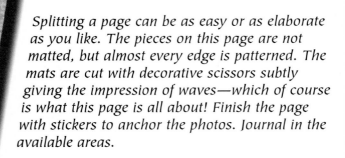

Splitting a page can be as easy or as elaborate as you like. The pieces on this page are not matted, but almost every edge is patterned. The mats are cut with decorative scissors subtly giving the impression of waves—which of course is what this page is all about! Finish the page with stickers to anchor the photos. Journal in the available areas.

Tropical Reef Patterned Paper: *Paper Pizazz™ Bright Great Backgrounds* by Hot Off The Press
Scissors: Bubbles Paper Edgers by Fiskars®, Inc.
Ruler: Déjà Views™ by C-Thru® Ruler Co.
Stickers: Frances Meyer Inc.®
Page Designer: Debbie Peterson

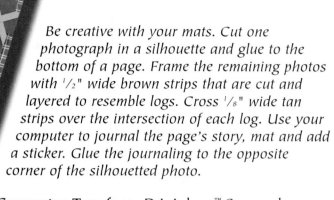

Be creative with your mats. Cut one photograph in a silhouette and glue to the bottom of a page. Frame the remaining photos with ¹/₂" wide brown strips that are cut and layered to resemble logs. Cross ¹/₈" wide tan strips over the intersection of each log. Use your computer to journal the page's story, mat and add a sticker. Glue the journaling to the opposite corner of the silhouetted photo.

Computer Typeface: D.J. Inkers™ Squared
Green Plaid Patterned Paper: Northern Spy
Stickers: Frances Meyer Inc.®
Page Designer: Kim McCrary for Pebbles in My Pocket

Some people look at bright or busy papers and think their photos won't show. Not so! Your photos will be even more special because they are on a background which reflects their theme. Glue a patterned paper offset on a plain paper and glue this angled to a 12"x12" page. Journal and embellish around the sides of the paper. Add the matted photos, then apply stickers over and around them. Glue the die cut at the page top.

Patterned Paper: Frances Meyer Inc.®
Cheers Die Cut: Ellison® Craft & Design
Stickers: Frances Meyer Inc.®
Page Designer: LeNae Gerig for Hot Off The Press

By itself, this photo doesn't have much of a "story"; skillful journaling and paper selection present a clear theme for the day's events. Create an elegant mat by using stationery. Mat again on plain paper and place at the top left of the page. Cut a wave strip and glue to the lower page. Use the anchor die cut, stickers and journaling to balance the page. (Anchor pattern on page 140.)

Stationery: Frances Meyer Inc.®
Scissors: Stamp Paper Edgers by Fiskars®, Inc.
Anchor Die Cut: Ellison® Craft & Design
Seagull Stickers: ©Mrs. Grossman's Paper Co.
Page Designer: Bridgette Server for Memories & More™

© & ™ Ellison® Craft & Design

Letters from *Paper Pizazz™ Black & White Photos*

Glue a 2" wide green strip down one side of the page. Cut the letters patterned paper into individual letters. Place the polka dot paper at an angle over the large letters on the right side. Place yellow cardstock torn on two sides over the dot paper. Insert smaller letters under the yellow paper. Continue layering the different elements until you are satisfied. (Eiffel tower pattern on page 141.)

Letters Patterned Paper: *Paper Pizazz™ Black & White Photos* by Hot Off The Press
White Dot on Red Patterned Paper: *Paper Pizazz™ Ho Ho Ho!!!* by Hot Off The Press
Corner Cutter: Elegance Corner Edgers by Fiskars®, Inc.
Stickers: Melissa Neufeld Inc.
Flag & Eiffel Tower Die Cuts: Ellison® Craft & Design
Silver Pen: ZIG® Opaque Writer by EK Success Ltd.
Page Designer: Stephanie Taylor

When designing pages, it is important to realize how the page will be viewed. This page's bright journaling draws the eye immediately. Photos at the corners draw the eye outward, then further outward to explore the photos between them. The shells are converted from the background to a page element by using the craft knife to cut around the shells, then inserting the photos into the slits.

Sand & Shells Patterned Paper: *Paper Pizazz™ Our Vacation* by Hot Off The Press

Scissors: Ripple Paper Edgers by Fiskars®, Inc.

Craft Knife: X-acto® by Hunt

Red, Blue and Black Pens: ZIG® Writer by EK Success Ltd.

Page Designer: Becky Goughnour for Hot Off The Press

Mat green paper on tan paper. Crop the path from the forest path patterned paper and glue a silhouetted photo into it as if the figure is "in" the paper. Mat on brown and glue to the top of the page. Double-mat the other photos on a plain paper and the remaining forest path paper. Cut four corners from the forest path paper and glue the elements to the page. Add journaling in the empty area.

Forest Path Patterned Paper: *Paper Pizazz™ Masculine Papers* by Hot Off The Press

Green Handmade and Tan Handmade Patterned Papers: *Paper Pizazz™ Handmade Papers* by Hot Off The Press

Oatmeal Handmade Patterned Paper: *Paper Pizazz™ Solid Muted Colors* by Hot Off The Press

Corner Cutter: Art Deco Corner Edgers by Fiskars®, Inc.

Scissors: Deckle and Heartbeat Paper Edgers by Fiskars®, Inc.

Page Designer: Debbie Peterson

Forest Path from *Paper Pizazz™ Masculine Papers*

When making a two-page spread, use similar elements on both pages. The double-mat around the outside edges combines these pages into one, allowing plenty of room for the large die cut headline. Similar matting techniques complete the effect. Notice how the bucket die cut balances the sun die cut.

Striped and Tan Handmade Patterned Papers: Paper Patch®
Scissors: Jumbo Deckle by Family Treasures
Bucket, Letter, Shovel and Sun Die Cuts: Ellison® Craft & Design
Page Designer: Kim Skinner for Memory Lane

© & ™ Ellison® Craft & D

© & ™ Ellison® Craft & Design

Sometimes there is no obvious theme for patterned papers. This is the time to get creative! Choose paper colors that compliment the colors in the photos. Angle the gold sheet on a patterned sheet. Cut off the corners and use them in the blank corners. Mat the photos on a third paper and place on the page. Journal with a contrasting pen—in this case, silver.

Gold Swirl Patterned Paper: *Paper Pizazz™ Bright Great Backgrounds* by Hot Off The Press
Metallic Dots and Metallic Gold Patterned Papers: *Paper Pizazz™ Metallic Papers* by Hot Off The Press
Corner Cutter: Corner Rounder by Marvy® Uchida
Silver Pen: ZIG® Opaque Writer by EK Success Ltd.
Page Designer: Katie Hacker for Hot Off The Press

This unique cropping technique begins by cropping a photo in a rectangle, then cutting off one corner. It provides plenty of room for journaling and is a great effect for this sea-scape page. Use the pattern (see 142) to cut the seaweed at the lower page. Arrange the page elements, adding stickers among the seaweed and photos. Leave large portions of the page blank to accent the background paper.

Scissors: Ripple Paper Edgers by Fiskars®, Inc.
Green & Blue Reef Patterned Paper: *Paper Pizazz™ Bright Great Backgrounds* by Hot Off The Press
Stickers: ©Mrs. Grossman's Paper Co.
Page Designer: Debbie Peterson

When possible, use colors representative of the place you vacationed. The colors on this page are bright and festive—like a piñata. The small stickers create a background while the larger stickers and die cut provides focal points. The scissors used to mat the photos are geometrical and vaguely Southwest in design completing the effect.

 Computer Typeface: D.J. Inkers™
 Scissors: Aztec Paper Edgers by Fiskars®, Inc.
 Sombrero Die Cut: Ellison® Craft & Design
 Stickers: ©Mrs. Grossman's Paper Co.
 Page Designer: Bridgette Server for Memories & More™

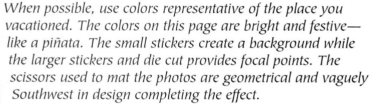

© & ™ Ellison® Craft & Design

When you have many photos of the same event, combine a group shot with an individual photo of each person. Mat and arrange them on the page, using the group shot as the focal point. Journal under each photo. Add a corner arch on two sides to provide journaling space for the whole page.

Brown Plaid Patterned Paper: *Paper Pizazz™ Great Outdoors* by Hot Off The Press
Oatmeal Handmade Patterned Paper: *Paper Pizazz™ Solid Muted Colors* by Hot Off The Press
Scissors: Deckle Paper Edgers by Fiskars®, Inc.
Corner Template: Border Corner Arch by Keeping Memories Alive
Page Designer: Debbie Peterson

Vacations almost always feature a trip to "somewhere," so make the destination the star of a page! Silhouette several spectacular scenic photos, mat each separately and layer onto a page. Add a group picture at the bottom of the page to showcase the area and who went. Journal the date in a blank area. For these photos, the matting was torn around the rocks to create extra jagged edges.

Clouds Patterned Paper: *Paper Pizazz™ Vacation* by Hot Off The Press
Red Corrugated Patterned Paper: *Paper Pizazz™ Country* by Hot Off The Press
Page Designer: Becky Goughnour for Hot Off The Press

Often, you will have a favorite picture from a trip that deserves special treatment. Mat the photo on gray and use silver and black pens to embellish the edges. Mat the gray on yellow, then glue at an angle to a 12"x12" gray page. Journal and add stickers on the outer gray paper and around the edges of the yellow mat to create a theme. The French journaling hints as the locale. Add enough stickers so the paper looks patterned rather than plain.

Oval Template: Provo Craft®
Silver Pen: ZIG® Opaque Writer by EK
   Success Ltd.
Stickers: The Gifted Line®
Page Designer: Stephanie Taylor

Centering the elements make it easy for the viewer to understand this page. Write individual letters on plain paper and cut them out. The irregular sizes, shapes and angles of the rectangles add interest. Mat the photo and glue it to the lower center of the page. Mat the letters on plain paper, outline with a pen and glue them above and below the photo as shown.

Red and Black Plaid Patterned Paper: *Paper Pizazz™ Great Outdoors* by Hot Off The Press
Page Designer: Sherri Johnston for Pebbles in My Pocket

Portraits & Pets

There are two categories of photos that require special treatment: portraits and pets. Portraits, while capturing the physical appearance of a person, often fail to convey the personality of the soul. Many times, pictures of our pets suffer from the same problem. So, we have grouped them here—as unrelated as they may seem—to show you ideas of how to express the true character of the photographed subject through the use of technique and memory album tools— die cuts, punches and papers!

Die cuts, an excellent time-saving embellishment, warmly express the emotions three friends share at the bottom of page 124. As you can see, adding penned details to the die cuts make them even more effective. The page at the top of page 122 uses many die cuts of the same shape, but different sizes arranged on the page to create an explosion of stars, stripes and dots that suggest there's more to this boy than a quiet, demur smile.

Creative use of punches can give your portraits the novelty they deserve. The album page at the top of page 121 sprinkles many heart punches on the page. Combined with the contrasting background paper and the soft flowers on the photo mat, a feel of love and tenderness coupled with fun and spontaneity is created. Still another expressive use of memory album tools comes at the bottom of page 125. Here, decorative scissors and a round punch were combined to depict a woolly lamb. The playful angle of the lamb's head and ears indicate the character of the pet.

Patterned papers offer almost endless opportunities to express personality traits. The sunflower garden paper used behind Bailey at the top of page 125 implies his eagerness for outdoor fun. The leopard paper behind Mallory on at the bottom of page 127 is an appropriate background for the shots of her stealthy prowess! For every theme, memory album tools have your ideas in mind! In fact, it would be a challenge for you to find a photo they couldn't enhance!

The border for this section was created using a corner punch from Family Treasures.

The flower and lace papers on this page work well with the women's flower dresses. Cut four corners off the daisy paper using plain scissors. Mat on dark green trimming with decorative scissors. Trim the laser lace paper and place under each corner. Triple-mat a picture, using plain and decorative scissors, then glue it to the center of a pattered sheet. Place the mother saying Punch-Out™ under it.

Laser Lace from
Paper Pizazz™
Romantic Papers

Impressionist Daisies, Laser Lace and Pink Hydrangeas Patterned Papers: *Paper Pizazz™ Romantic Papers* by Hot Off The Press

Mother Saying Punch-Out™: *Paper Pizazz™ Sayings Punch-Outs™* by Hot Off The Press

Scissors: Colonial Paper Edgers by Fiskars®, Inc.

Page Designer: Katie Hacker for Hot Off The Press

A mother holds her children's hands for a while, their hearts forever.

Before beginning, lay your photo on several different papers. Choose a color that duplicates the colors in the photo or emphasizes a background element. The hydrangeas paper is a great start, but the page needs contrast. The yellow paper matches Ashton's outfit. The mats underneath it help to combine the background, mat and photo. The purple sponge paper used for a mat is used for the journaling along with yellow mats and lette to complete this coordinated page.

Antique Laces and Purple Sponged Patterned Papers: *Paper Pizazz™ Pretty Papers* by Hot Off The Press

Hydrangeas Patterned Paper: *Paper Pizazz™ Very Pretty Papers* by Hot Off Th Press

Scissors: Deckle Paper Edgers by Fiskars® Inc.

Alphabet Stickers: Frances Meyer Inc.®

Page Designer: Stephanie Taylor

Portrait pages don't have to be elaborate to be spectacular. This romantic yet easy page can be accomplished with a patterned paper and a punch. Glue the photo to the center of a piece of stationery. Mount on a coordinating plain paper. Punch many white hearts and glue them all over the plain paper. Journal on a separate piece of paper and glue below.

Stationery: idesign greetings
Heart Punch: Family Treasures
Page Designer: Sherri Johnston for Pebbles in My Pocket

One of the most elegant portrait designs is multiple matting. This page makes wonderful use of varying mat widths, tying them together by using complimentary colors and the roses cut from the background paper.

Rose Stationery: Frances Meyer Inc.®
Corner Cutter: Corner Rounder by Marvy® Uchida
Page Designer: Amber Blakesley for Paper Hearts

This vibrant page says a lot without even trying! Notice how the yellow mat separates the portrait from the background paper while the dotted mat ties the elements together. The die cut stars provide color and journaling space as well as decorative elements. The firecrackers suggest this picture might have been taken around the fourth of July—or at least in the summer.

Red and White Stripes Patterned Paper: *Paper Pizazz™ Christmas Time* by Hot Off The Press
White Dots on Red Patterned Paper: *Paper Pizazz™ Ho Ho Ho!!!* by Hot Off The Press
Firecracker and Star Die Cuts: Ellison® Craft & Design
Page Designer: LeNae Gerig for Hot Off The Press

© & ™ Ellison® Craft & Des

© & ™ Ellison® Craft & Design

Though black and white photos often look good with some color, you can make a truly striking page using black, white and gray papers. This swirl patterned paper, with its many shades of gray, offsets the high contrast pictures. The pictures are matted first on black paper, then on light gray which is still darker than the swirl. Use a gold pen to journal on black and cut out the journaling. Glue the photos, journaling and black corners to the page, being careful to balance the elements so one page area is not heavier than another.

Black & White Swirl Patterned Paper: *Paper Pizazz™ Black & White Photos* by Hot Off The Press
Gold Calligraphy Pen: Marvy® Uchida
Page Designer: Amberly Beck

This white-on-white, layered die cut frame accents the photo's soft, tinted colors. The die cuts are kept from blending together by adding pin marks around the edges of some shapes, adding texture. The green page frame echoes the darker backgrounds. The bright journaling and chick stickers draw the eye to the page corners, ensuring the viewer will notice the page's details.

Colored Pencils: Berol Krismacolor
Heart and Star Die Cuts: Ellison® Craft & Design
Stickers: ©Mrs. Grossman's Paper Co.
Page Designer: Sandi Genovese for Ellison® Craft & Design

The black and white mats are a lovely beginning, but they need more contrast to draw interest. The flowers add a touch of color to soften this striking page. Adding the stickers in the corners is a final touch, linking the picture to the flower mat.

Black & White Check, Black & White Gingham and Summer Flowers Patterned Papers: Paper Patch®
Stickers: Melissa Neufeld, Inc.
Page Designer: Allison Myers for Memory Lane

Use an 8¹/₂"x11" paper to make a 12"x12" page by drawing the paper onto the blank areas. Offset mat a large portrait and cut the shells from the paper covered by the photo. Use these shells and scallop punches as embellishments around the page, gluing them in the blank areas as shown. Leave the upper left corner relatively bare to unbalance the page and draw the eye to other plain areas. This is a nice effect and provides a smart use of extra paper.

Shells Patterned Paper: *Paper Pizazz*™
   Vacation by Hot Off The Press
Scallop Punch: Marvy® Uchida
Page Designer: Stephanie Taylor

© Expressly Portraits

Die cuts provide quick and easy frame material—just take the time to draw on them before gluing. Add other repeated elements, such as the outlined letters glued in front of a plain colored set to create a shadow. Place a single rose and sticker in the lower left corner to add a special detail.

Soft Rose Patterned Paper: NRN Designs
Lettering Template: Pebbles ABC Tracer
   by Pebbles in My Pocket
Pink and Green Pens: ZIG® Clean Color
   by EK Success Ltd.
Rose and Flower Die Cuts: Ellison® Craft &
   Design
Sticker: R.A. Lang Card Co.
Page Designer: Heather Hummel

Pet Pages

Your pets are just as important as your children or spouse. Here are six great ideas to showcase the "other" members of your household.

Ever wondered how to get your favorite pet story on a page without having a huge block of journaling? Run the story around a wide mat! Combined with a favorite picture of this reluctantly clean pooch, the story adds insight into Bailey's character. Don't be afraid to experiment with different journaling styles, taking your inspiration from the examples shown on pages 18–23 of this book. This country-dot journaling looks spectacular with the bright papers used for matting. The sunflowers in the corners of the red with dots paper are cut from the background sheet.

Red with Dots Patterned Paper: *Paper Pizazz*™
Bright Great Backgrounds by Hot Off The Press
Sunflower Garden Patterned Paper: *Paper Pizazz*™
Little Charmers by Hot Off The Press
Page Designer: LeNae Gerig for Hot Off The Press

It isn't necessary to detail every action to create a clear story on a page. Careful photo selection, clever use of shapes and journaling accomplish what thousands of words cannot! The sheep's heads and bodies are ovals cut with scalloped scissors to create a "wooly" effect. The eyes are punched from the head with a round punch. The feet are ovals cut with regular scissors. The free form swirls fill the empty areas like so many bubbles!

Bubbles Patterned Paper: *Paper Pizazz*™ *Baby* by Hot Off The Press
¼" Round Punch: McGill, Inc.
Scissors: Deckle and Scallop Paper Edgers by Fiskars®, Inc.
Page Designer: Debbie Peterson

Pet pages make some of the best memory album pages because there is something about our pets that makes us smile. This page successfully combines two patterned papers of the same color. One is simply matted at an angle with the corners trimmed. Capture the "joy" of a bath with journaling arranged on a hose—complete with water coming out! Glue the Punch-Outs™ dripping from the hose and place the matted photos between the drops and the hose. (Hose pattern on page 139.)

Blue Streaks and White Squiggle on Blue Patterned Papers: *Paper Pizazz™ Bright Great Backgrounds* by Hot Off The Press
Drop Punch-Outs™: *Paper Pizazz™ Holidays & Seasons Punch-Outs™* by Hot Off The Press
Page Designer: LeNae Gerig for Hot Off The Press

Some pets don't "do" a lot, but they are still an important family member. Make a page about the pet's diet or daily activities, using paper to subtly add to the theme. Hedgehogs eat bugs, so use a bug paper to mat your photos. Add a journaling comment or small story to let the viewer know what your pet is like.

Bugs on Screen Patterned Paper: *Paper Pizazz™ Great Outdoors* by Hot Off The Press
Grass Patterned Paper: *Paper Pizazz™ Pets* by Hot Off The Press
Scissors: Volcano Paper Edgers by Fiskars®, Inc.
Page Designer: Katie Hacker for Hot Off The Press

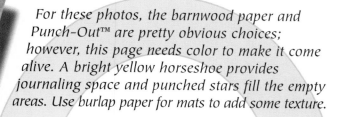

For these photos, the barnwood paper and Punch-Out™ are pretty obvious choices; however, this page needs color to make it come alive. A bright yellow horseshoe provides journaling space and punched stars fill the empty areas. Use burlap paper for mats to add some texture.

Barnwood and Burlap Patterned Papers: *Paper Pizazz™ Country* by Hot Off The Press
Horsin' Around Punch-Out™: *Paper Pizazz™ Sayings Punch-Outs™* by Hot Off The Press
Scissors: Scallop Paper Edgers by Fiskars®, Inc.
Star Punch: McGill, Inc.
Page Designer: Katie Hacker for Hot Off The Press

A day in the life of any cat shows many zany activities and leopard paper shows your cat's wild side! Offset the leopard paper on black. Embellish the black edges and journal on black with the gold pen. Mat the photos on gold. Mat the large journaling on two shades of brown. Arrange as shown, using the pattern below and a circle punch to make the kitty paw beside the journaling as a finishing touch.

Leopard Patterned Paper: Frances Meyer Inc.®
Metallic Gold Paper: *Paper Pizazz™ Metallic Papers* by Hot Off The Press
¹/₂" Circle Punch: Fiskars®, Inc.
Gold Pen: ZIG® Opaque Writer by EK Success Ltd.
Page Designer: Becky Goughnour for Hot Off The Press

Black & White

In a world of colorful detail, the simple beauty of striking contrast can be lost. Maybe that's why our black and white photos are so special. This chapter provides ideas to create an album page that will give your black and whites the respect they demand.

The use of laser-cut lace paper offers a distinctive feel no matter how its placed. The couple at the top of page 133 is beautifully framed by lace corners, while the use of lace at the bottom of the same page forms a timeless bridge over youth and the ages. Lace showcases the photo of Becky at the top of page 137 and elegantly accents the antique feel of the "wall paper" pattern behind it.

Distinctive matting techniques create unique pages. The top album page on page 130 has triple-matted photos on contrasting paper. After adding elaborate gold embellishments, these photos are gracefully matted a fourth time. The lower album page uses four different matting techniques to produce the depth that this elegant photo deserves.

The album page at the top of page 132 uses polka dots and crooked numbering to echo the playfulness of the 1940's. The album page at the top of page 134 uses strong primary colors as its background to reflect the "Yes, I can" attitude of the new generation. The gentle outdoor colors used behind the photo at the bottom of page 135 hint at the colors we don't see, making their absence even more powerful. The smooth look of leather behind the photos at the top of page 136 offer a distinguished characteristic that unmistakably says "Gentleman."

Though void of color, Black & White photos are not without character, and by exploring the techniques in this chapter you can illustrate the times of your own life and your ancestors.

The border for this section was created using
Colonial Paper Edgers by Fiskars®, Inc.

Old fashioned papers and accents work well with black and white photos. Trim a piece of hydrangeas paper with decorative scissors and glue to the center of the antique laces paper. Triple-mat each photo on plain papers that bring out its highlights. Use the cherub and ribbons cutouts to decorate the photos as shown. Mat the embellished photos again with pink paper before gluing them to the page.

Antique Laces and Hydrangeas Patterned Papers: *Paper Pizazz™ Pretty Papers* by Hot Off The Press
Metallic Silver Paper: Hygloss Products, Inc.
Bow and Cherub Cutouts: *Paper Pizazz™ Embellishments* by Hot Off The Press
Scissors: Majestic Paper Edgers by Fiskars®, Inc.
Page Designer: Debbie Hewitt

Though this page combines four matting techniques, this elaborate design is easier to create than you might think. Mat a photo on plain tan and punch the corners. Mat on purple moiré, then make ¹/₄" wide slits ¹/₂" apart around the mat. Weave ribbon through them. Mat on the antique laces paper, trim and glue to plain purple paper. Self-adhesive lace strips are matted on paper and placed on four sides of the photo.

Antique Laces and Purple Moiré Patterned Papers: *Paper Pizazz™ Pretty Papers* by Hot Off The Press
Scissors: Colonial Paper Edgers by Fiskars®, Inc.
Corner Cutter: Corner Rounder by Marvy® Uchida
Corner Cutter: Family Treasures
Craft Knife: X-acto® by Hunt
Lace: Wrights®
Ribbon: C.M. Offray & Son, Inc.
Page Designer: Anne-Marie Spencer for Hot Off The Press

Photo corners complement older photos. Corner punches are another way of making photo corners. Punch your mat or use the punched shape to anchor your photos. On this page, pre-cut photo corners are mixed with two different corner punches.

Burgundy Handmade Patterned Paper:
  Paper Pizazz™ Handmade Papers by Hot Off The Press
Tapestry Patterned Paper: *Paper Pizazz™ Pretty Papers* by Hot Off The Press
Corner Cutters: Family Treasures
Photo Corners: Canson®
Page Designer: Allison Myers for Memory Lane

Using similar colors, styles and elements on facing pages creates a coordinated look. On these pages, each photo is matted in the same colors and the same corner punch is used. Each page's journaling is done in the same font and matted in the same shape. The final connecting touch is provided by stickers.

Corner Cutter: Family Treasures
Stickers: The Gifted Line®
Page Designer: Karen McGavin for Pebbles in My Pocket

There are many clever tricks to make your pages interactive. One is a pull-out, such as on this page. Make your page as usual, mounting the film strip on double-sided foam tape and leaving a large space at the lower right for the pull-out. In the empty space, glue one end of a folded die cut or a 4"x11" rectangle with seven ½" folds in the center. Glue 1943 to the outside of the fold-out. Glue silhouetted pictures to the inside folds. Add a sticker and new date inside. Insert the page into a sheet protector and cut the casing over the pull-out. (Film strip pattern on page 142.)

Red with White Dots Patterned Paper:
  Paper Patch®
Borderline: ©Mrs. Grossman's Paper Co.
Folded Pull-Out, Film Strip and Number
  Die Cuts: Ellison® Craft & Design
Stickers: ©Mrs. Grossman's Paper Co.
Page Designer: Sandi Genovese for Ellison®
  Craft & Design

These light photographs really stand out with red mats on a black background. The light journaling paper balances the photos, keeping the page from leaning one way or the other. The white rectangle in the upper right corner is actually a clear pocket, containing tee die cuts and real blades of grass for keepsakes! Use an envelope die cut to cut a clear sheet protector and tuck the grass and tees into it.

Golf Ball Patterned Paper: Paper Pizazz™ Sports by Hot Off The Press
Alphabet, Envelope, Golf Ball and Tee Die Cuts: Ellison® Craft & Design
Heart Stickers: ©Mrs. Grossman's Paper Co.
Press-On Letters: LetterEase by Ellison® Craft & Design
Page Designer: Sandi Genovese for Ellison® Craft & Design

Sepia tone photographs look best when matted with soft, golden tones rather than bright colors or black and white papers. This page makes good use of dark and light papers. Mat the photo on a paper that is light enough to contrast the dark background, yet dark enough to show up against the light-colored flooring. Triple-mat on crushed suede, gold swirl and plain brown paper. Add the cutout under the photo. Cut the laser lace into four pieces as shown and glue one to each corner.

Crushed Suede and Brown & Gold Swirl
Patterned Papers: *Paper Pizazz™ Black & White Photos* by Hot Off The Press
Laser Lace: *Paper Pizazz™ Romantic Papers* by Hot Off The Press
"1905" Cutout: *Paper Pizazz™ Black & White Photos* by Hot Off The Press
Scissors: Colonial Paper Edgers by Fiskars®, Inc.
Page Designer: Anne-Marie Spencer for Hot Off The Press

If you use tinted photos, choose papers to bring out their color. Trim the photo and mat on yellow roses paper. Mat again on diagonal ribbons paper, trim and mat on plain yellow paper. Glue ³/₄" wide yellow roses paper strips to the top and bottom of the page. Cut apart the laser lace and glue around the top and bottom of the page, using the largest pieces first and inserting the smaller pieces as shown.

Diagonal Ribbons and Yellow Roses
Patterned Papers: *Paper Pizazz™ Romantic Paper* by Hot Off The Press
Laser Lace: *Paper Pizazz™ Romantic Papers* by Hot Off The Press
Scissors:
Colonial Paper Edgers by Fiskars®, Inc.
Page Designer: Anne-Marie Spencer for Hot Off The Press

Laser Lace from *Paper Pizazz™ Romantic Papers*

Diagonal Ribbons from *Paper Pizazz™ Romantic Papers*

Color can be used with black and white photos just as it can be with regular photos, though brighter colors tend to work better with true black and white photos. As always, try to stick to two or three colors rather than trying to work the entire rainbow into your page.

Letter Die Cuts: Ellison® Craft & Design
Scissors: Ripply by McGill, Inc.
Stickers: Frances Meyer Inc.®
Striped and ABC Patterned Papers: Frances Meyer Inc.®
Page Designer: LeNae Gerig for Hot Off The Press

Determine the contrast of the photo before beginning. Light photos look good on dark pages with lighter contrasts. This photo has a light background; it will look best on a black mat. Mat again on white, then place on a dark page. Journal on a light color and use the same matting techniques. Add contrasting embellishments with a dash of color for interest.

Black with White Dots Patterned Paper: Paper Patch®
Daisy Die Cut: Pebbles in My Pocket
Page Designer: Erika Clayton for Pebbles in My Pocket

May 1991 - erika & jessica
Not very often does a friend like Jessica come around. Since the 7th grade we've been inseperable. We've spent countless hours giggling, crying, sharing secrets, and our dreams for the future- which include to live next door to each other. But no matter where we live- she will always be in my heart.

This striking page is very easy! Mat the photos on red, then on the black and white check paper. Glue to a black page and add red corners. Finally, place on checked paper. **Hint:** *Cut out the center of the checked sheet and use it for the mats before gluing the black sheet to it.*

Black and White Check Patterned Paper: Paper Patch®
Rose Die Cut: Ellison® Craft & Design
Page Designer: Karen McGavin for Pebbles in My Pocket

© & ™ Ellison® Craft & Design

Skyline Homecoming 1997
Spencer Dent asked me to the dance with a poster that said "How would you like to ROLO in Homecoming with this Babe." (There was a picture of him as a baby). I had to go through a package of ROLO candies to find his name. We had a great time!

Double-mat the photos, leaving a 1/2" plain paper margin to journal on. Glue at an angle to a contrasting sheet of paper. Punch many white flowers, yellow circles and red hearts. Glue the yellow circles to the flowers. Place the flowers around the picture in groups of 2–5, using a few single flowers to fill empty areas. Place the hearts under and beside the flowers. Arrange until satisfied, leaving the largest groups at the corners. Glue, then connect the groups with penned vines.

Green & White Check and Yellow & White Gingham Patterned Papers: Paper Patch®
1/2" Circle Punch: Family Treasures
Flower and Heart Punches: Marvy® Uchida
Page Designer: LeNae Gerig for Hot Off The Press

He Loves me • He Loves me Not • He Loves me

135

When you need inspiration for your album pages, look around! This page was inspired by an old leather-bound book. Trim a piece of crushed suede paper to 6³/₄"x9¹/₄". Mat once on dark brown and again on tan before matting on leather paper. Use the ribbon to "wrap" the corners as shown. Mat your photos on gold and black and glue to the page. Journal in old-fashioned script and you have a page to begin any family album!

Crushed Suede Patterned Paper: *Paper Pizazz™ Black & White Photos* by Hot Off The Press
Leather Patterned Paper: *Paper Pizazz™ Masculine Papers* by Hot Off The Press
Metallic Gold Paper: *Paper Pizazz™ Metallic Papers* by Hot Off The Press
¹/₄" **wide Tan Satin Ribbon:** Wrights®
Page Designer: Becky Goughnour for Hot Off The Press

The corrugated paper is a great start to this page for two reasons—it is interesting, but not distracting, and the seam bringing the two sheets together is completely indistinguishable. The black paper is cut into large, geometric shapes and matted on gray. The gray is embellished with a ●—●— border and the pieces are layered as shown. The photo is glued to black paper trimmed with a rotary cutter. Double-mat on gray and white, adding a ●•●• border to the white mat.

Red Corrugated Patterned Paper: *Paper Pizazz™ Country* by Hot Off The Press
Scalloped Rotary Cutter: Fiskars®, Inc.
Page Designer: Stephanie Taylor

Starting with a white mat allows these black and white photos to work on pastel paper. The thin black mats echo the black journaling and roses' outlines. Matting the laser lace on pink allows it to show well against the patterned background, completing the rather old-fashioned look of this page. With thought and care there is nothing you can't do with black and white photos!

Tri-dots on Pink Patterned Paper: *Paper Pizazz™ Light Great Backgrounds* by Hot Off The Press
Watercolor Roses Patterned Paper: *Paper Pizazz™ Very Pretty Papers* by Hot Off The Press
Laser Lace: *Paper Pizazz™ Romantic Papers* by Hot Off The Press
Scissors: Deckle Paper Edgers by Fiskars®, Inc.
Page Designer: Becky Goughnour for Hot Off The Press

Mat the white satin paper on white and use border stickers around the edge. Crop the photo into a 4³/₄" tall oval and cut the muted roses paper into an 8" oval. Glue the photo to the lower center of the rose paper. Glue to the page and use stickers around the photo and paper edge. Be sure to use larger stickers around the outside, placing the largest at the top.

Muted Roses and White Satin Patterned Papers: Paper Pizazz™ Wedding by Hot Off The Press
Stickers: The Gifted Line®
Page Designer: Stephanie Taylor

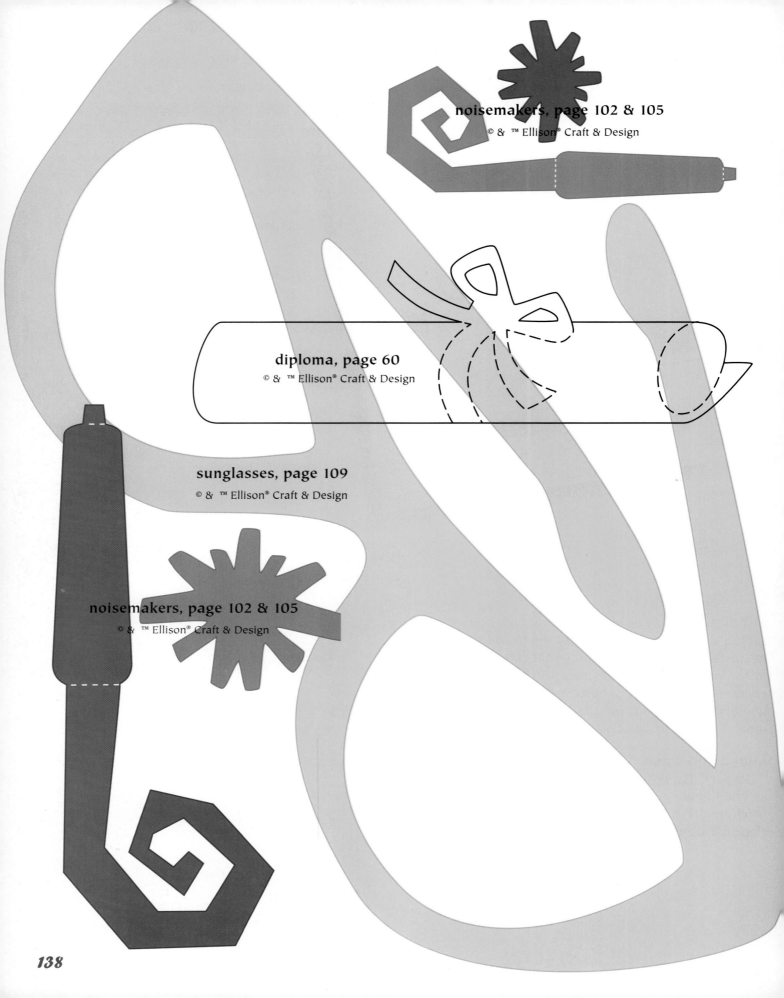

noisemakers, page 102 & 105
© & ™ Ellison® Craft & Design

diploma, page 60
© & ™ Ellison® Craft & Design

sunglasses, page 109
© & ™ Ellison® Craft & Design

noisemakers, page 102 & 105
© & ™ Ellison® Craft & Design

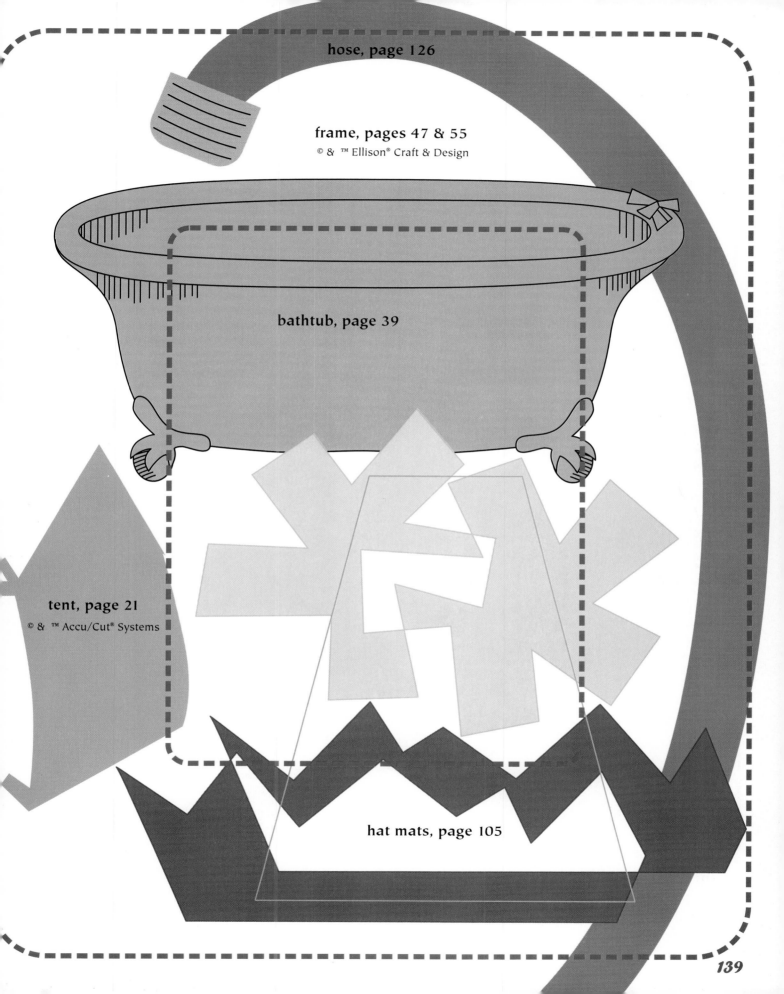

hose, page 126

frame, pages 47 & 55
© & ™ Ellison® Craft & Design

bathtub, page 39

tent, page 21
© & ™ Accu/Cut® Systems

hat mats, page 105

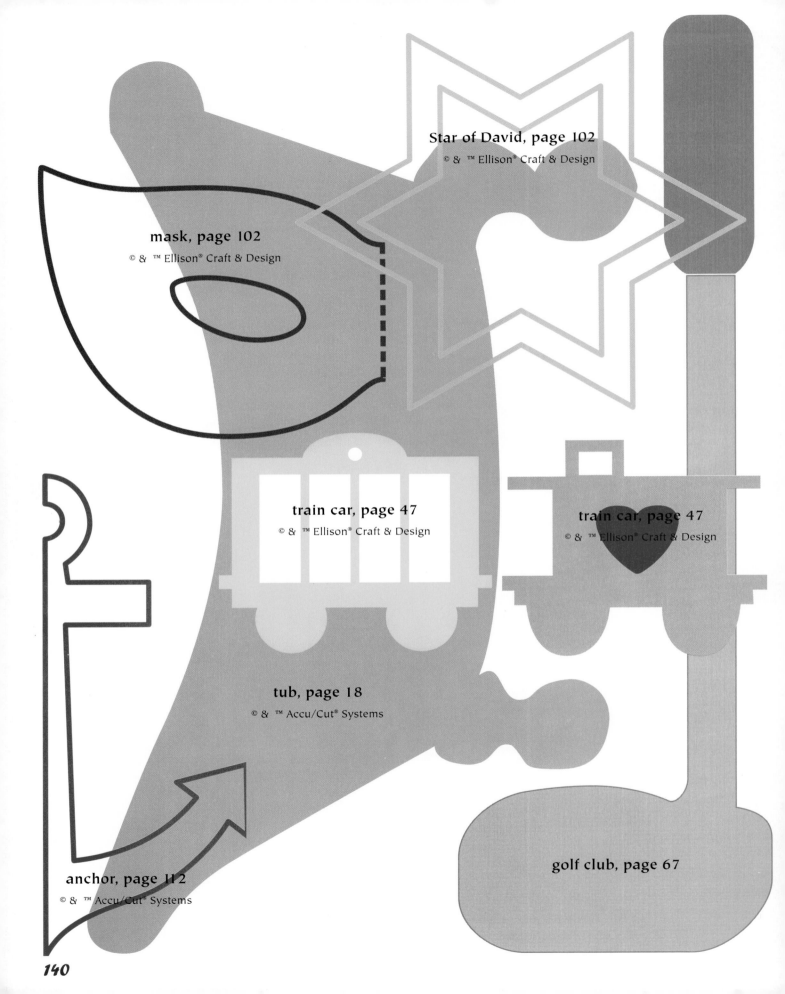

Star of David, page 102
© & ™ Ellison® Craft & Design

mask, page 102
© & ™ Ellison® Craft & Design

train car, page 47
© & ™ Ellison® Craft & Design

train car, page 47
© & ™ Ellison® Craft & Design

tub, page 18
© & ™ Accu/Cut® Systems

anchor, page 112
© & ™ Accu/Cut® Systems

golf club, page 67

140

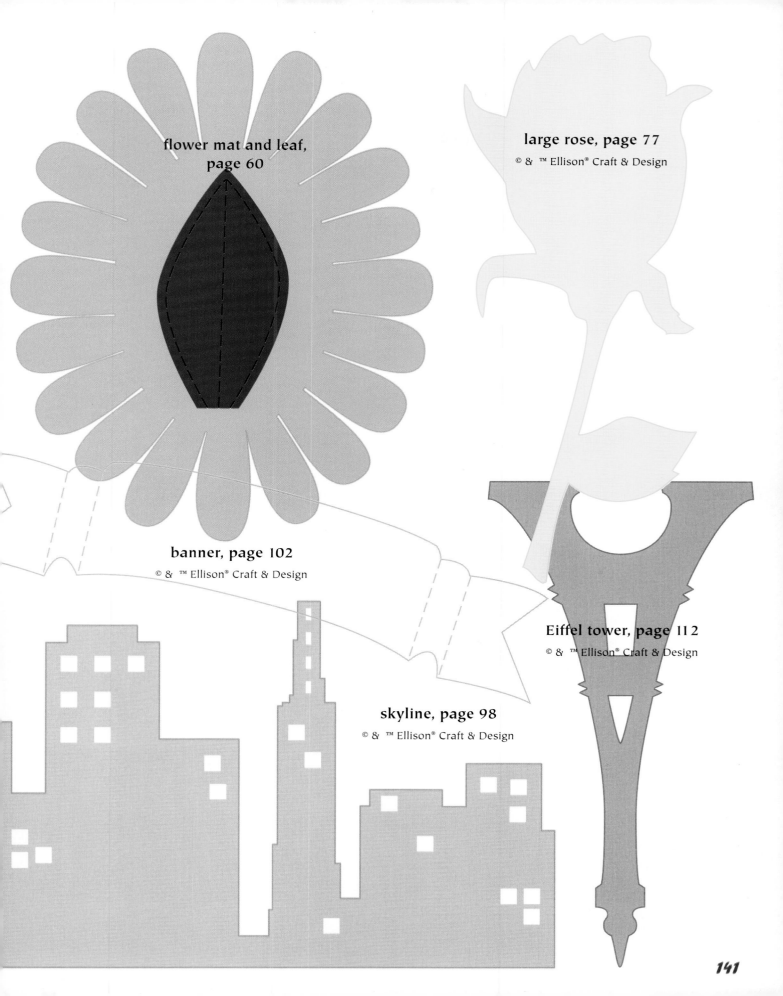

flower mat and leaf,
page 60

large rose, page 77

© & ™ Ellison® Craft & Design

banner, page 102

© & ™ Ellison® Craft & Design

Eiffel tower, page 112

© & ™ Ellison® Craft & Design

skyline, page 98

© & ™ Ellison® Craft & Design

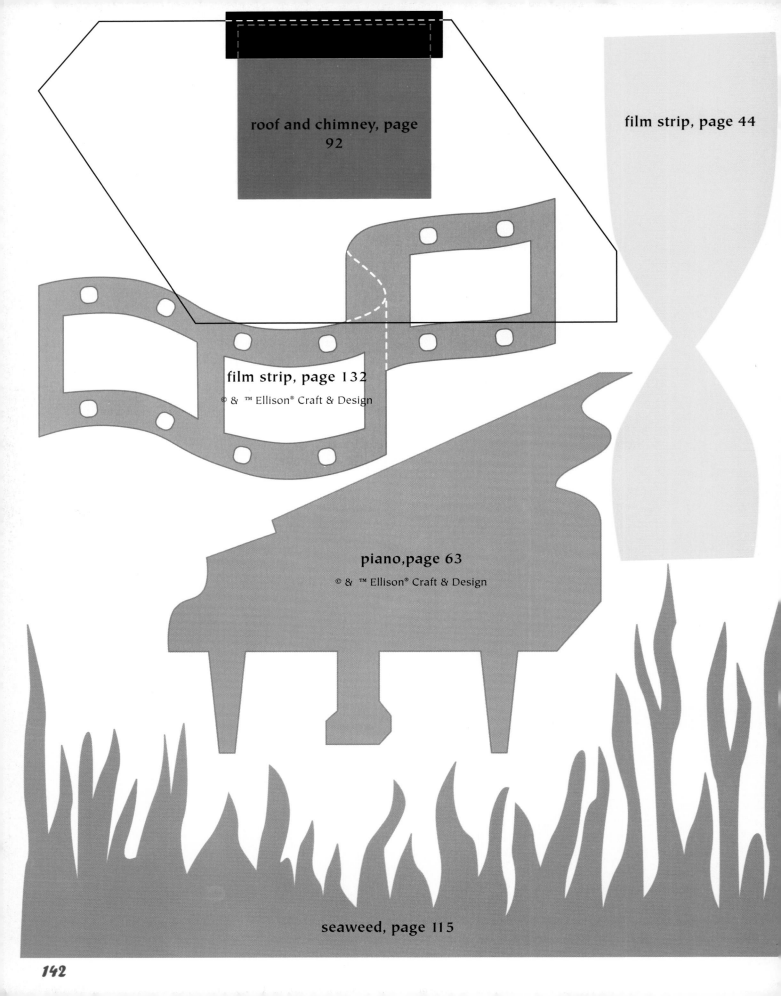

roof and chimney, page 92

film strip, page 44

film strip, page 132

© & ™ Ellison® Craft & Design

piano, page 63

© & ™ Ellison® Craft & Design

seaweed, page 115

Acid-free
Acid is used in paper manufacturing to break apart the wood fibers and the lignin which holds them together. If acid remains in the materials used for photo albums, the acid can react chemically with photographs and accelerate their deterioration. Acid-free products have a pH factor of 7 to 8.5. It's imperative that all materials (glue, pens, paper, etc.) used in memory albums or scrapbooks be acid-free.

Acid migration
is the transfer of acidity from one item to another through physical contact or acidic vapors. If a newspaper clipping were put into an album, the area it touched would turn yellow or brown. A de-acidification spray can be used on acidic papers, or they can be color copied onto acid-free papers.

Archival quality
is a term used to indicate materials which have undergone laboratory analysis to determine their acidic and buffered content.

Buffered Paper
During manufacture a buffering agent such as calcium carbonate or magnesium bicarbonate can be added to paper to neutralize acid contaminants. Such papers have a pH of 8.5.

Cropping
Cutting or trimming a photo to keep only the most important parts. See page 14–15 for cropping ideas and information about cropping Polaroid photos.

Imprintables
A term used in the stationery market for papers which have a plain center and a design on the border. With the center empty, the paper can be printed on for party invitations or announcements.

Journaling
refers to the text on an album page giving details about the photographs. Journaling can be done in your own handwriting or with adhesive letters, rub-ons, etc. It is probably the most important part of memory albums. See pages 18-23 for more information.

Lignin
is the bonding material which holds wood fibers together as a tree grows. If lignin remains in the final paper product (as with newsprint) it will become yellow and brittle over time. Most paper other than newsprint is lignin-free.

pH factor
refers to the acidity of a paper. The pH scale is the standard for measurement of acidity and alkalinity. It runs from 0 to 14 with each number representing a ten-fold increase; pH neutral is 7. Acid-free products have a pH factor from 7 to 8.5. Special pH tester pens are available to help you determine the acidity or alkalinity of products.

Photo-safe
is a term similar to archival quality but more specific to materials used with photographs. Acid-free is the determining factor for a product to be labeled photo-safe.

Sheet protectors
These are made of plastic to slip over a finished album page. They can be side-loading or top-loading and fit 8½"x11" pages or 12"x12" sheets. It is important that they be acid-free. Polypropylene is commonly used—never use vinyl sheet protectors.

Sources

Manufacturers & Suppliers

Accu/Cut® Systems
1035 E. Dodge St.
Fremont, NE 68025

All Night Media®, Inc.
Post Office Box 10607
San Rafael, CA 94912

C.M. Offray & Son, Inc.
Route 24, Box 601
Chester, NJ 07930

Creative Card Company
1500 W. Monroe
Chicago, IL 60607

D. J. Inkers™
Post Office Box 2462
Sandy, UT 84091

C-Thru® Ruler Co.
6 Britton Dr.
Bloomfield, CT 06002

EK Success Ltd.
611 Industrial Rd.
Carlstadt, NJ 07072

Ellison® Craft & Design
Toll Free 888-972-7238
714-724-0555

Embossing Arts Co.
3196 Rolland Dr.
P.O. Box 439
Tangent, OR 97389

Extra Special Products Corp.
Post Office Box 777
Greenville, OH 45331

Family Treasures, Inc.
24922 Anza Dr., Unit D
Valencia, CA 91355

Fiskars® Inc.
7811 W. Stewart Avenue
Wausau, WI 54401

Frances Meyer Inc.®
Post Office Box 3088
Savannah, GA 31402

Hot Off The Press, Inc.
1250 NW Third, Dept LA
Canby, OR 97013

Hygloss Products, Inc.
402 Broadway
Passaic, NJ 07055

idesign greetings
12020 W. Ripley Ave.
Milwaukee, WI 53226

Keeping Memories Alive™
260 N. Main
Spanish Fork, UT 84660

Making Memories™
Post Office Box 1188
Centerville, UT 84014

Marvy® Uchida
3535 Del Amo Blvd
Torrance, CA 90503

McGill, Inc.
Post Office Box 177
Marengo, IL 60152

Melissa Neufeld Inc.
6940 Koll Center Parkway, Suite 100
Pleasanton, CA 94566

MPR Associates, Inc.
529 Townsend Avenue
High Point, NC 27263

Mrs. Grossman's Paper Company
Post Office Box 4467
Petaluma, CA 94955

NRN Designs
5142 Argosy Ave.
Huntington Beach, CA 92649

Provo Craft®
285 E. 900 South
Provo, UT 84606

Rubber Stampede®
Post Office Box 246
Berkeley, CA 94701

Sakura of America
30780 San Clemente St.
Hayward, CA 94544

Suzy's Zoo
9401 Waples St.
San Diego, CA 92121

The Gifted Line®
1-800-5-GIFTED
FAX 510-215-4772

The Paper Patch
Post Office Box 414
Riverton, UT 84065

Wrights®
85 South Street
West Warren, MA 01092

Retail Stores:

Memories & More™
CA, UT, CO, NV
1-800-286-5263

Memory Lane
700 E. Southern Avenue
Mesa, AZ 85204

Paper Hearts
6185 Highland Dr.
Salt Lake City, UT 84121

Pebbles In My Pocket
1132 S. State St.
Orem, UT 84058

144   The borders in this section were created with a corner punch from Family Treasures.